TOPOGRAPHICAL MEMOIR

The published writings of Captain Cram detailing the deaths of south-
western Oregon Indians at the hands of U.S. Army officers and volunteers were received with anger and we trust, shame. However attention is
called to an error in line 15, page 40, which states that only one (white)
man survived the battle at Battle Rock, Port Orford. Actually all nine
white men who took part in the affair survived. The battle started June
10, 1851. It was several days before the men reached a safe location.

Of this edition _250_ copies were printed.

This is Copy Number _105_.

TOPOGRAPHICAL MEMOIR

THOMAS JEFFERSON CRAM

YE GALLEON PRESS
FAIRFIELD, WASHINGTON
1977

Library of Congress Cataloging in Publication Data

United States. Army. Corps of Topographical Engineers.
Topographical Memoir.

Reprint of the 1859 ed. published by U.S. Army Corps of
Topographical Engineers, Washington, which was issued as Ex. doc.
no. 114 of the 35th Congress, 2nd session, House of Representatives;
with new introduction.
1. Pacific States—Description and travel. 2. Pacific
coast—Defenses. 3. Pacific Coast Indians, Wars with, 1847-1865. I.
Cram, Thomas Jefferson, 1807?-1883. II. Title. III. Series: United
States. 35th Congress, 2nd session, 1859. House. Executive document;
no. 114.
F851.U59 1977 979'.02 77-15634
ISBN 0-87770-193-8

INTRODUCTION

Thomas Jefferson Cram was a professional soldier, one of the many military officers who helped bring the refinements of white culture to the American west in the 1840's and 1850's, decades when thousands of white-topped covered wagons were crawling west on the Oregon Trail and the California Trail. He served through the Civil War rising steadily in rank to be brevetted a brigadier-general and major-general in 1866 for his service in that bloody conflict.

He was born about 1807 in New Hampshire and became a cadet at the United States Military Academy, West Point, July 1, 1822, from which he was graduated July 1, 1826, brevetted Second Lieutenant, Second Artillery. He stood fourth in a class of forty-one at West Point and was given a place on the faculty as assistant professor of mathematics, 1826-1829, and of natural and experimental philosophy, 1829-1836. He resigned from the West Point faculty at that time and worked as an engineer on railroads in Pennsylvania and Maryland for the next two years. He returned to the U.S. Army in 1838 with rank of Captain and served as topographical engineer on several surveys. In 1845 and 1846 he was an officer making military reconnoissances in Texas. From 1855 to 1858 he was chief topographical engineer, Department of the Pacific. In these years he accumulated material and impressions which were written into his *Topographical Memoir*, now a fairly rare book. His humanitarian views toward native Americans did not endear him to civilian authorities whose goal was the rapid extinguishment of Indian title to land they had lived on for hundreds of generations. Thomas Jefferson Cram, still a Captain, served on the staff of General Wool in the P.N.W. Territorial Governor Isaac Ingalls Stevens was engaged in a running feud with General Wool and the writings of Captain Cram, published in eastern newspapers did nothing to dampen these flames. Still loyal to his commander, Cram, now a Lieutenant-Colonel, served as aide-de-camp to General Wool in 1862 in the campaign to capture Norfolk, Virginia. Following the Civil War Cram, now with the brevet rank of Major-General, served on engineering boards for improvement of harbors on the Great Lakes. He was retired on February 22, 1869. Death came in Philadelphia on December 20, 1883. The feud between Territorial Governor Isaac I. Stevens and General John E. Wool, who was head of military forces on the Pacific Coast in 1855-56, and in which Captain Cram played a considerable part . . . is today difficult to describe. It was obviously a conflict between civilian and military authority and of course a conflict of personalities. Isaac Stevens had a civil position as governor of Washington Territory, newly formed in 1853, but he actually wore three hats as he was in charge of a survey for the Northern Pacific Railroad, and he was empowered to make treaties with Indian tribes in his area. Stevens was an 'empire builder' determined to bring immediate civilization to the Pacific Northwest wilderness of the 1850's. Stevens, a former military officer serving in a civilian position, was behaving like an officer and ordering people around. Crusty General John E. Wool did not take kindly to this sort of treatment. Wool was a gentleman of the old school, born in the late 1700's, he believed that treaties with Indians should be respected. Isaac Stevens was determined to open the interior of Washington Territory to white settlement even though Congress had not ratified the Walla Walla treaty of 1855, and did not do so until after the Wright-Steptoe campaigns of 1858. Of course the Indians had been paid nothing for their lands and such important groups as the Coeur d'Alenes and Spokanes had made no treaty with the U.S. Government.

Isaac Stevens in most autocratic fashion had declared martial law following the Indian war of 1855 in the Puget Sound lowland. Stevens was particularly vindictive toward Indian Chief Leschi and offered a reward for his capture. Unfortunately Leschi was betrayed and tried on a charge of murder at Steilacoom. The jury disagreed, however on a second trial Leschi was convicted. There was strong feeling against Leschi, the theoretical leader of the Indian uprising and it is questionable if a fair trial could have been had in the area in which he lived, nevertheless many just men felt that after the conclusion of the war many matters were best forgotten and that the execution of Leschi was not good judgment.

General John E. Wool protested that greed of the whites was primarily responsible for the Indian war and that the war was encouraged by men who favored the use of unnecessary volunteer soldiers, who were supplied with food, horses and equipment at high prices, in the hope that these 'debts' would be honored by the federal treasury. Wool also charged the volunteer forces, with outrageous conduct, violence, murder, not without some justification. General Wool also ordered Colonel George Wright to arrest Governor Stevens, which order Wright wisely ignored. Stevens also ordered the arrest of a judge who had displeased him. General Wool was unfavorably impressed by the semi-desert interior of Washington Territory and felt it best left to the Indians, to whom it obviously belonged, a point of view which of course outraged the empire builders and displeased the whites who wanted free land and were interested in farm lands, mineral wealth and timber, none of which were of much interest to the nomadic native peoples who occupied this land.

Governors Curry of Oregon and Stevens of Washington made formal complaint against General Wool and eventually got him transferred out of the P.N.W. Despite their acid opinion of John E. Wool this crusty old officer served with distinction in the Civil War and accomplished far more than Isaac Stevens who met death in fool hardy fashion at the minor battle at Chantilly. It might be fairly said that Isaac Stevens, of towering ambition and great personal courage, was a man ahead of his day; where John E. Wool, born in the previous century, was out of date and perhaps out of place. Captain Cram in saying a few words in defense of native peoples was writing sincerely but on a subject highly unpopular in the mid-nineteenth century when to impatient and greedy whites the only good Indian was a dead Indian. John Beeson, possibly the first white man to come to the defense of native Americans in the P.N.W., was nearly lynched in Oregon and had to go east to get his book on the subject printed. Historian Thomas W. Prosch of Tacoma as late as 1915 felt that 'every copy' of Captain Thomas Jefferson Cram's *Memoir* should be 'suppressed by fire.'

It may be noted that Secretary of War Floyd, while disapproving of the views of Captain Cram, did order the Cram report to be printed. It is reprinted today on the chance that it may be of mild interest to serious students of Pacific Northwest history.

Glen Adams
Fairfield, Washington
September, 1977

INDIAN CRADLE, WASHINGTON TERRITORY

TOPOGRAPHICAL MEMOIR OF THE DEPARTMENT OF THE PACIFIC.

LETTER

FROM

THE SECRETARY OF WAR,

TRANSMITTING

The topographical memoir and report of Captain T. J. Cram, relative to the Territories of Oregon and Washington, in the military department of the Pacific.

MARCH 3, 1859 —Laid on the table, and ordered to be printed.

WAR DEPARTMENT, *March* 3, 1859.

SIR: I transmit herewith the report of Captain T. J. Cram, Topographical Engineers, on the military department of the Pacific, called for by a resolution of the House of Representatives.

The topographical information contained in this report is, to a great extent, published in the reports and maps of the War Department, or is in course of preparation.

A large portion of the report is devoted to subjects irrelevant to its objects, as indicated by the title and the duties of Captain Cram, and contains animadversions upon public functionaries, which are out of place in a topographical communication, and which are, in no sense, sanctioned or endorsed by this department.

Very respectfully, your obedient servant,

JOHN B. FLOYD,
Secretary of War.

Hon. JAMES L. ORR,
Speaker of the House of Representatives.

WAR DEPARTMENT,
OFFICE OF EXPLORATIONS AND SURVEYS,
Washington, February 24, 1859.

SIR: I transmit herewith the military topographical memoir and report, with maps, on the military department of the Pacific, by Captain T. J. Cram, Topographical Engineers, called for by a resolution of the House of Representatives of January 8.

This is the report to which I called the special attention of the War Department in a report dated March 1, 1858.

Very respectfully, your obedient servant,

A. A. HUMPHREYS,
Captain of Topographical Engineers, in charge.

Military topographical memoir and report, with maps, * on the United States military department of the Pacific, by Thomas Jefferson Cram, captain Corps of Topographical Engineers, chief topographical engineer, department of the Pacific, 1855, '56, '57.*

PREFACE.

This memoir has been drawn up by virtue of orders received by me while serving in the department of the Pacific, under the command of Major General J. E. Wool, United States army, of which the following is a copy:

HEADQUARTERS DEPARTMENT OF THE PACIFIC,
Benicia, California, June 20, 1855.

SIR: The commanding general directs that you prepare a topographical memoir, or view of the department of the Pacific, and that, for this purpose, you consult such papers as may be on file at these headquarters. You will also call upon any officers serving within the department for such information as they may be able to give you in the execution of these instructions.

I am, sir, very respectfully, your obedient servant,

E. D. TOWNSEND,
Assistant Adjutant General.

Captain T. J. CRAM,
Topographical Engineers, Benicia, California.

Accordingly, the information herein embodied has been derived—
1. From reports, sketches, journals of marches by officers of the line, containing much that is valuable, and from reports of reconnaissances and maps by topographical engineer officers, as I found them at headquarters, without, however, having been, as it seemed

---

* The maps, not having been ordered by the Committee on Engraving, have not been printed.

to me, previously digested, arranged, and embodied in a useful shape for practical military purposes, before being forwarded to the War Department.

2. From conversations during personal interviews with many officers of the line and of the staff (too many to be here enumerated) who had been serving in various districts of the department, and who seemed to me to have intelligently calculated the resources of the country and various points of the different branches of the military service.

3. From my own personal observations upon the country, and upon the practical operations of the several branches of the service, during a tour of duty (of from two to three years) in various directions and at various places, and in various surveys and reconnaissances in the department in the years 1855, '56, '57, while in the performance of duties as senior topographical engineer officer, attached to the general staff of the commanding general of the department of the Pacific.

In drawing up the memoir and report I have not confined myself simply to the task of reporting topographical information, but have shaped all in a manner, while rendering much of that kind of information in the text and maps, so as also to meet the requisition contained in paragraph 481, Army Regulations; hence the double title of "Memoir and Report," seen on title page.

Therefore, it will be observed that this will contain what may be regarded as a report of the military and other operations connected with, or having relation to, the military service, as they came under my own observation; and it will likewise embrace my own views, as well as the views of other officers when relevant, in regard to various points, upon which it will be seen by those having the patience to follow me that I have freely, but I trust respectfully, commented in the ensuing chapters.

Not only shall I deem it within the scope of my province to report what I regard as existing evils in the working of the military operations of the regular army, and of the self-constituted volunteer armies that have been in the field in the department, and of the Indian service in its relations with the army, but I shall feel at perfect liberty to report suggestions which, from a source however destitute of pretension, might, if carried into effect, remove those evils, to the great benefit of the army service in the department of the Pacific.

I.—General description of the military department of the Pacific.

This department includes within its limits the State of California, the Territories of Oregon, Washington, and Utah, containing 718,367 square miles in surface; to use the language of one of its distinguished commanders, "altogether, in size, an empire of itself."

Map No. 1 represents its general features, as far as necessary for general description. The military posts, as now located, are named in red letters, and are 21 in number, viz: nine in California, four in

Oregon, eight in Washington, and none in Utah; others may have to be established to meet exigencies. The physical features of this great area, while eminently favorable to secure the Indians and the depredating whites from pursuit, are, in themselves, formidable obstacles to the transit of troops, with the necessary supplies for anything like an extended march into the interior of the country.

These physical obstacles consist in numerous ranges of lofty mountains, of great extent, with which the whole department is checkered; a comparative deficiency in the number and extent of navigable rivers; the want of suitable natural roads, and the extreme difficulty of making roads, owing to the formidable obstacles presented by the mountains all over the department, and, besides, the denseness of the forests in Oregon and Washington. The only physical feature at all favorable to military movements is the great extent of seacoast navigation, from the post of San Diego to that at Bellingham Bay, an extent of about 1,400 miles, which may be regarded as the sea front of the department.

Fortunately, this extensive front is furnished by nature with good harbors, viz: the Bay of San Diego at the south and the waters of Washington at the north; also one of the best in the world, at an intermediate point, in the Bay of San Francisco.—(See maps Nos. 7, 16, 2.) This bay, and the other smaller tide-water bays with which it is connected by navigable straits and channels, are surrounded by a shore extent of 200 miles; and they are navigable by sail and steam vessels in any direction, and their waters communicate with the ocean by a deep navigable strait, the "Golden Gate," inside of which stands the city of San Francisco.—(See map No. 2.)

With these beautiful bays two navigable rivers (the Sacramento and San Joaquin) communicate: the former, from the north, affording steamboat navigation at all stages to Sacramento, 129 miles above San Francisco, and at high stages 150 miles further up; the latter river, coming from the southeast, affording similar navigation to Stockton, 115 miles above San Francisco.

The Columbia is the only other river navigable for any extent piercing the ocean front of the department of the Pacific.—(See map 16.) But the circumstances of the bar at its mouth (see map No. 3) will forever preclude it from being a harbor. Nevertheless, this river, navigable, without interruption, up to the Cascades, 183 miles above its mouth, and in several reaches above that, and its tributary, the Willamette, (see map No. 14,) which also has navigable reaches separated by falls, are both important in reference to military lines of communication with the interior of the department.

The Straits of Fuca, and Washington waters generally, (see map No. 16,) forming an extent of navigation, by sail or steam, for some hundreds of miles, having connexion with the ocean front of the department, and having several excellent harbors, also possess highly important advantages for military movements interior to this front.

Again: the Colorado river of California, though not piercing this ocean front within our own possessions in the department, is nevertheless of military importance, (see map No. 7,) and it is used by us for military purposes, as far as it is known to be navigable by steamers, up to Fort Yuma, 125 miles above its mouth; and should the explorations now in progress prove it navigable higher up, it will become of still greater military importance to the department of the Pacific.

The foregoing named natural channels of interior communication are of too much importance to be overlooked by any officer connected with the military service in the department, and they should be carefully studied at the War Department, in every bureau, in reference to their adaptation and connexion with the seacoast front for military purposes, more especially as all other physical features of the whole interior, generally, are so adverse that these natural channels must forever exercise a controlling influence in almost all important operations to be carried on, whether in establishing posts, furnishing them with troops and supplies, or executing movements from the posts into the Indian countries. For this study, and for sufficiently minute detail in reference to these watercourses, maps and topography will be given in this memoir, all in their proper places, so as to cover the whole department.

From the general topography now given, and a study of map No. 1 alone, it seems to me it cannot fail to be perceived that, for the general military business of the department, whether in ordinary or extraordinary circumstances, the city of San Francisco necessarily becomes the principal and permanent centre of that business. Hence the great importance to the War Department of retaining the military reserve called Presidio, near that city, and of there erecting suitable buildings for a depot of troops and supplies, and constructing a public dock; hence the propriety of establishing, and the advantage of retaining, the headquarters of the department at San Francisco or the Presidio—an advantage too clearly to be seen from the general topography of the department, and the pre-eminent commercial character of the city, to need evidences of minor or collateral circumstances, of which, however, many could be adduced to sustain it.

The operations of an army must, and the centre of those operations likewise ever be subject, in a great measure, to the physical features of the country in which the forces are operating.

The business of carrying on military operations in a department requires labor, materials, and supplies, other than what can be furnished by the soldier or the officer. In the department of the Pacific labor will always be high, and materials likewise; these, in addition to the generally adverse physical features of the country, will necessarily cause all military operations to be very expensive—in a ratio of from $2\frac{1}{2}$ or 3 to 1 to what they would be under the same commander and the same set of staff officers in the department of the west; and it is well for the War Department, Congress, and the people, to be apprised of the reasons why it will be so.

Circumstances are so adverse to transit and locomotion generally in this department that the duties of all, whether of the line or staff, when called into the field or to move from one part of the country to another, become exceedingly difficult and often onerous; and none more so, for example, than those devolving on the pay officers, whose duties are not only arduous, but involve great pecuniary responsibility. The posts are remote, and the means of transportation uncertain. The routes to be travelled are, in some parts of the country, impassable during the winter or rainy season, the mountain passes entirely obstructed by snow, and the rivers unfordable. During the summer months the heat on the plains or deserts to be crossed in several of the routes is almost insupportable, and water extremely scarce.

The distance to be travelled by the paymaster stationed at headquarters, in paying the district under his charge, is 1,896 miles, a large portion of which being through a country infested by robbers and Indians. The southern pay district includes the posts at San Diego, Fort Tejon, and Fort Yuma, and the paymaster travels 900 miles, twice crossing a desert of 90 miles in making his periodical round. In Oregon and Washington the labor of the pay officer, with all the risks of a new and unsettled country, is by no means to be coveted. The posts within this district are widely scattered, the means of travelling even more precarious, and the seasons less favorable than in California. With all these impediments to this branch of the military service, it ought to be a subject of congratulation that thus far the treasury has sustained no loss, and the troops have been paid with much regularity in this department.

The same adverse circumstances operate forcibly to prevent the officers of the quartermaster's department from conducting their part of the military service so as to elicit from one unacquainted with these obstacles anything but encomium in respect to economy, while to one cognizant of the physical features of the country it would seem a matter of surprise how this class of officers generally manage, under such difficulties, with as much economy as they do.

To supply the troops with the necessary subsistence at the proper time in the various seasons, and of the proper quality, it must be confessed, requires no ordinary capacity in the chief of the commissariat in the department of the Pacific, especially when one considers the difficulties of communication, the vicissitudes of climate, and the comparatively few districts in which supplies are produced.

In the following chapters much will be found of practical utility for the foregoing classes of officers, in so far as the exercise of their official duties may be dependent on or influenced by the topographical features of the department.

II.—*Military considerations in reference to the ocean front of the department of the Pacific.*

This front, extending, as already stated, 1,400 miles, from San Diego to Bellingham Bay, has now established on it the following named posts: San Diego, Presidio, Humboldt, Umpqua, Port Townsend, Steilacoom, Bellingham Bay, all of which are occupied by troops.

These posts are generally accessible in all seasons from San Francisco by sail and steam vessels. At each, excepting Humboldt and Umpqua, a steamer is seldom prevented by stress of weather from entering port; fogs sometimes cause delay. With the exceptions mentioned, all may be said to possess good harbors; that of Humboldt requires lighterage, except for vessels of small draught, and that of Umpqua is difficult to enter except under the most favorable circumstances.

There are two other points on the sea front to which, although not military posts, some military importance attaches under the circumstances existing in the department—San Pedro, to the south, and Crescent City, to the north of San Francisco—as ports at which troops and supplies are landed for interior posts.

The United States mail steamers run semi-monthly from San Francisco to or by all the points above named excepting Port Townsend, Steilacoom, and Bellingham Bay, regulating their times of departure and return by those of the United States mail steamers from San Francisco for New York. In regard to the posts at Port Townsend, Steilacoom, and Bellingham Bay, a mail steamer communicates from one to the other monthly, the central point of departure of which is at Olympia, the capital of Washington Territory. With this town there is mail communication semi-monthly, (from San Francisco,) *via* the Columbia river, to Rainier; thence, *via* Cowlitz river and overland, to the said centre of departure.

At all times movements of troops and of supplies by sea in the department are attended with great expense, and at any other time than that corresponding to the starting of the mail steamers with still greater expense, as a steam vessel has to be expressly chartered. Still it is only by such a vessel that a given point can be reached in a specified time to meet exigencies; and, as a general rule, experience has shown in the past three years that trusting to sail vessels for this branch of the military business has been attended with more expense, including damages by long voyage, than by employing steamers whenever occasion has required a movement of troops and the transportation of a large quantity of stores from San Francisco to any of the points named.

When the time of delivery is unimportant, and the quantity of supplies and number of troops quite small, then a sail vessel may possibly be used with some saving; but in no other case should any but a steam vessel be used if true economy be sought.

Distances and times by sea steamers.

From—	To—	St. miles.	Days.
San Francisco	Post San Diego	450	2.1
	San Pedro	320	1.5
	Fort Humboldt	258	1.2
	Crescent City	320	1.5
	Fort Umpqua	464	2.1
	Mouth of Columbia	783	3.6
	Cape Flattery	793	3.7
	Fort Port Townsend	900	4.2
	Fort Steilacoom	1,008	4.7
	Fort Bellingham Bay	923	4.3

In the foregoing table the times of steaming from San Francisco to the several points are computed at a sea-steamer speed of 9 statute or 7.87 nautical miles per hour, and the table gives a fair average of the times observed in the trips of the transport steamers now engaged in that coast navigation.

From San Francisco, *via* Los Angeles, it is 434 miles to San Pedro, and 537 to San Diego, following the road, which is excellent all the way, and over which a large body of troops, with its wagon train, could make good marching time. On this part of the coast, which is south of San Francisco, there are several points at which from an enemy's fleet the landing of an invading foe, if undisputed, could be readily effected; but should it attempt a march upon San Francisco there would be found many points on the road where the topography teaches us that a resolute body of well-disciplined defenders, of comparatively small numbers, well doing their duty, as was the case at Buena Vista, could annihilate an advancing column, or effectually check the demonstration of a much larger force, and compel it to seek its safety in retreat to its ships, or to make a detour into the valleys of the Sierra Madre, the Coast range, (see map No. 4;) and here, if one or two passes be properly defended, an invasion could never be effectual upon San Francisco, nor could it reach into the heart of the State of California. A description of these passes will be given in another chapter. To carry San Francisco, the enemy would thus be compelled to attack it with its fleet.

The time is very remote, if it should ever come, when the southern part of the State of California will be in a condition to invite an enemy to attempt to hold possession of that part of it; but if he should gain a temporary position there he would be dislodged by a field force; accordingly, there is no reason why our government should ever expend a dollar in erecting seacoast fortifications between San Francisco and San Diego. Should this last point, however, become a commercial place, or the terminus of a railroad to the Pacific, a permanent fort here might be requisite. But the time for this must be placed in the remote distance of events to come.

With regard to the coast of the department north of San Francisco, there is no road at all running along it upon which troops could operate except in small bodies, and then transportation must be made by pack-trains. This condition holds all the way to the Columbia river, thence to Cape Flattery, also between the posts in Washington Territory; nor will there ever be, in our day, a continuous coast road upon which a command could march, with a suitable wagon train, for the whole or even a tenth part of the distance. Passable military roads, however, may be opened from a few points on this part of the coast to extend back into the interior. No march of a body of troops landed from an enemy's fleet would ever be attempted in a direction parallel to this coast, nor will there ever be anything in the interior of this most forbidding stretch of country to induce the movement of such a force into the interior should a reasonable show of defence be exhibited by a field force. And it may be affirmed, with good reason, that there is no point on the coast of the department north of San

Francisco, or even on the banks of the waters of Washington Territory, where the construction of permanent forts, for at least three generations to come, would be anything but an extravagant waste of the public treasure.

In making this declaration I am well aware of encountering an opposite opinion of an ex-Secretary of War, who has reported to Congress, through the President, that "the physical geography of the vast region drained by the Columbia river indicates that at some day a great city must arise at the point which shall become its commercial entrepôt. Attention has been heretofore called to the necessity of fortifying the entrance of the Columbia river, and I would again commend it to attention and favorable consideration."

It is not on account of the future greatness here predicted for the "vast regions drained by the Columbia" that I have quoted this somewhat extraordinary paragraph, but it is in reference to the military point therein contained that I have called it up for notice. If its author had studied the chart by the United States Coast Survey, (see map No. 3,) which was published before the recommendation was made, I doubt if he would ever have come to any such opinion as that of a "necessity," or even of there being a possibility of defending the mouth of the Columbia with any known practical system of fixed batteries. Nature has already fortified this entrance in a manner to preclude the necessity of man's adding to the defence, except by floating batteries.

The minimum breadth of the mouth of the Columbia is $6\frac{1}{2}$ miles, from Point Adams to Cape Hancock. Within this the channels vary in position, in depth, and in crookedness. The mouth is always blocked by a mass of oscillating sand, called the "Bar." In the channels, at high tide, a vessel drawing 18 feet can seldom pass the bar. These channels are tortuous, and from ten to fifteen miles in length, and no vessel attempts to enter or emerge in stormy or rough weather; they are emphatically fair weather channels only, and very dangerous at that. Owing to the oscillations of the sand eastward and westward, northward and southward, the channels are continually shifting their positions, shapes, and depths, necessitating the constant presence of a corps of pilots to observe them.

The vertical depth of the blockading sand is over 420 feet before any bottom could be met upon which to build a fortification, and at that depth even we are not certain of finding a stratum fit for foundations. It is true there is a middle ground, "Sand island," but this, as its name imports, is but a sand deposit, liable to wash away at any freshet; and I think it would be impossible to render it permanent. From this sand bank to Point Adams it is $2\frac{3}{4}$, and $3\frac{1}{2}$ miles to Cape Hancock. No works could be built on the sand shoals in the river to stand one season, and the channels are beyond the range of guns on the shores, if we except, perhaps, the north one, in its present position; but of what use would a fort be on that shore when there are two other ship channels each far beyond the reach of any battery on shore?

To one who has seen the Straits of Mackinaw and studied the question of fortifying them, and not seen the mouth of the Columbia, I would observe that the idea of fortifying the latter is more utopian than that of permanent fortifications at the former.

It must be by your fleet being outside of the bar in the open sea to give the enemy battle, or else in the river, some three to ten miles up from the bar, there to wait, allowing the enemy's ships to enter and then giving battle, that the command of the Columbia is to be retained; and this last method could be ventured upon with a small defending fleet by being in positions to attack the enemy's ships in detail, as they would never be able to enter either channel with more than one small vessel at a time.

It must also be by means of naval defence that the command of the waters in Washington Territory is to be retained, and not by any theoretical system of permanent works of fortification. Steam floating batteries are the weapons for these waters.

With regard to the military and commercial centre (see map No. 2) of the coast of the department of the Pacific it is different. Here the "Golden Gate" is eminently susceptible of defence by permanent forts; and whatever difference of opinion may exist in reference to the expediency of fortifying other points, none can exist in reference to the wisdom of fortifying with land batteries the entrance through the "Golden Gate" to San Francisco, to the fullest extent of perperfection, as speedily as the condition of time requisite for the solidification of the masonry will permit, notwithstanding the enormous cost to the treasury.

The Golden Gate well fortified, with a full armament faithfully served, also a few passes in the Coast range well defended by field forces, no invading force could seize upon the commercial centre of that coast, or successfully penetrate the heart of the department of the Pacific.

III.—*Military considerations in reference to the valleys of the Sacramento and San Joaquin rivers.*

In the chapter immediately preceding, the seacoast, and certain views in reference to its defence against a foreign enemy, have been presented, without special consideration of the districts interior to the ocean front. In this chapter (III) I present an interior view of so much as relates to the above named valleys, in so far as the topography of their features is necessary to enable the War Department, its bureaus, and the officer serving in the department of the Pacific, to realize the physical character of the country, so far as that character will exert more or less influence upon the military operations that may be carried on in it. This chapter will also contain, in connexion with the description of the valleys, some views in reference to a certain line of policy that has obtained, and the practical effect it has had upon the military service in the department for the past three years.

The lower portion of the valley of the Sacramento may be regarded as being occupied by a succession of beautiful bays, which are represented on map No. 2. Beginning with the uppermost, we have the Suisun bay, fifteen miles long by seven wide; this is connected by the Carquinez strait, of four miles in length, with San Pablo bay, fifteen miles long by eight wide; then comes a short channel connecting the last named bay with San Francisco bay, which is forty miles in length by eight miles in average width.

These bays are bordered by magnificent slopes of most excellent soil, and their shores have a multitude of excellent landings for the steam and sail vessels navigating these waters. Into and from these waters ships of large class enter and depart through the Golden Gate.

To the importance of San Francisco in a military aspect I have already alluded; its importance as the emporium of the east shore of the north Pacific is too well known to need comment. Its pre-eminent advantages as a military and commercial point are well attested in the facts that our government is fortifying the gate with works to defend it under any circumstances; that it has commenced a navy yard on Mark island, (see map No. 2,) in contemplation to be completed on a formidable scale, already furnished with ample floating dry docks which are of very great use to the naval and commercial marine in the Pacific; and that it has also established on the Carquinez strait, (see map No. 2,) just above Benicia, an arsenal, magazines, and a depot for army supplies.

In reference to the defensible works in contemplation to be completed for the gate I have spoken in chapter II.

In regard to the navy yard, there are certain cogent reasons that may be urged against its being allowed to grow into an establishment possessing the capacity for anything more than the conveniences requisite for repairing all kinds of war and merchant vessels. To bring it to this condition an appropriation of money would be true economy, but to foster its growth to a capacity for ship building upon a large scale would be wasting the public treasure. The forests that are accessible in the department do not afford timber or lumber of quality requisite for the construction of ships, excepting some of an indifferent quality for spars and yards procurable in Washington Territory. The absence of other raw and manufactured materials necessary for ships, and the high price of labor, and last, though not least, the want of an export trade, must, for a long time to come, operate to prevent ship building to any extent on our Pacific coast.

The question was entertained, if not originated, by the late Secretary of War, (and possibly the idea may yet be entertained in the ordnance department,) of enlarging the present arsenal near Benicia into an "arsenal of construction of the largest class." Progress has been so far made in the project as the ordering of a board of officers to report upon a suitable site, to be on the present reserve, and their report has been rendered for the enlargement contemplated.

But the wisdom of appropriating money for executing this design may reasonably be doubted, for the total destitution of that coast of all the chief materials essential for ordnance purposes would necessitate their transportation around the Horn; this, together with the high price of mechanics' labor, at once shows that it will be easier, cheaper, and better, to construct all munitions of war to be used on the Pacific coast in eastern arsenals, and transport them ready made, than first to transport the raw materials of so gross a nature and afterwards fabricate them at an "arsenal of construction in the department of the Pacific;" besides, the project would be attended with a dead loss of dollars in the excess of original outlay for the necessary buildings, tools, and machinery, over the cost of a similar establishment at any favorable location east of the Mississippi.

But of the policy of erecting on the present ordnance site (which is on the reserve) ample magazines for ammunition, storehouses for an abundance of ordnance and small arms, a convenient laboratory and shops for repairs, and a suitable dock, and a road from it to the buildings, there can be no doubt.

The works should partake of the character of an ordnance depot and an arsenal for repairs, rather than of an "arsenal of construction of the largest class."   This last is but the name which would afford the excuse for annually demanding heavy appropriations under which would grow up a national armory or national foundry in a portion of our country in which there is a remarkable destitution of all the essential elements entering into the things required to be made in such an establishment.   Suitable wood, iron, and coal for such purposes are as yet undiscovered in the department of the Pacific.

The public reserve near Benicia is well adapted for such an establishment as herein recommended for ordnance purposes and magazines for ammunition.

But in reference to the adaptation of this reserve for a depot of commissary and quartermaster's supplies and stores, it is exceedingly inappropriate.

All such supplies as are purchased, under army regulations, in San Francisco, have to be shipped from this place to Benicia, a distance of 30 miles, unloaded upon a dock, carted up a steep hill, unloaded into the storehouses, inspected, and then, what is not rejected, has to be carted back to the dock, reshipped upon another vessel, retransported to San Francisco, where it was when purchased, and there again transhipped for its distribution to the various posts.   Now, as might be expected, such complexity enhances the cost of the supplies by at least from 5 to 10 per cent. more than if inspected where they are purchased, and shipped, as they are wanted, directly to the various posts; and when it is observed that 18 out of the whole number of 21 posts participating in purchases at San Francisco have been supplied in that complicated manner, it will be an easy problem for the commissary department to compute the annual amount thus unnecessarily burdened upon the army appropriation by a pertinacious perseverance in a system that, for the past two to three years to my knowledge, has been the subject of severe comment and condemnation in the mouths of hundreds of highly respectable business men in that department.

Witness the facts shown in evidence before a court-martial for the trial of an officer of the commissariat, that during a period of some months, in which the troops were engaged in suppressing Indian troubles, the extra cost to the treasury was many thousand dollars, consequent upon the location of the commissary depot; and provision merchants of the highest standing testified in evidence before the court that their bids for supplies ranged from 5 to 10 per centum above what they would have been could the inspection have been made in San Francisco in lieu of Benicia.

Pending the investigation of the forenamed board upon the arsenal site, it was carefully estimated by one of the members that all the buildings on the reserve, used as storehouses and for other purposes by the quartermaster's and commissary's departments, could be rebuilt out of new materials for less than $20,000; I am satisfied this is a liberal estimate of the whole value, at the present time, of all the depot buildings there. The argument, therefore, that because these shells of buildings cost the government so much as they did to erect them they should be retained as a depot falls to the ground; better that they should burn than to entail such an annual tax, as their present use necessitates, upon the army appropriations.

True economy, in this respect, would be to utterly abolish what is now maintained at such great cost on the reserve under the title of "quartermaster's and commissary's depot," and the appendages of mule teams, vessels, horses, mechanics, and other employés would be dispensed with. The excuse of necessity can no longer be reasonably pleaded for keeping up this cumbersome establishment, which has come to be viewed by business men as anything but an economical appendage to the military service in the department.

The best economy for the present would be to hire, in San Francisco, the requisite storeroom, for which there are, convenient to docks, scores of most excellent buildings now vacant, and, as it were, begging for tenants; but in due time to erect all such buildings at the Presidio as may be needed for this important branch of the service in the department.

Having considered the bays of the valley of the Sacramento in reference to their adaptation for military and naval purposes for all future time, I pass to the consideration of the greater part of the valley to the north of Suisun bay, (see map No 1.) The Sacramento river is wholly within the department of the Pacific, and it has been thoroughly explored; its general course is south, and it debouches into Suisun bay, (see map No 2.) Although this river is neither very large nor very long, it is of great importance, and in most respects holds the first rank among the few navigable streams on the east border of the north Pacific. It is at all times successfully navigated by steam to the city of Sacramento, 75 miles above its mouth, and 150 miles further up (to Red Bluffs) in high stages of water. This beautiful river is to California what the Hudson is to New York.

Tributary to it is the Feather river, which enters the Sacramento

24 miles above Sacramento city, and is navigable 20 miles up to Marysville, a town of importance near the mouth of the Yuba, which is a tributary to Feather river.

The sources of the Sacramento and headwaters of its tributaries from the east and north are high up in the west slope of the Sierra Nevada mountain range; and here it is for a great extent along the foot of this slope, in thousands of places. Gold abounds to an extent which has astonished and delighted the whole civilized world for the past ten years. This, however, is not the only region in the department of the Pacific where it exists. It may be truthfully said it abounds in many places all over the department. On the Sierra slope the digging and washing of so much dirt to obtain it may affect the Sacramento, by the vast quantities of earth washed from multitudes of diggings into it, so as in time to seriously impair, if not to destroy, its navigation. The present indications are, that this earthy matter is being deposited in the bays.

The extensive valley of the Sacramento, and the lesser valleys of its tributaries, afford many fertile regions of soil of excellent quality for all agricultural purposes; this and the gold deposits are causing thriving towns, villages, and even cities to arise as if by magic. The climate has various phases as we go further from the coast into the interior, and as we ascend to different elevations on the mountain's side; and although fever and chills are known on the streams, it is generally pronounced a good climate.

The San Joaquin river, likewise, debouches into Suisun bay near where the Sacramento enters, and drains an extensive tract called Tulare valley, in which there is a vast deal of most excellent soil, though there is much of a low and mashy nature. The general course of the stream is northwestward, coming from the southeastern extremity of the Sierra Nevada. The river is navigable for steamers up to Stockton, 78, 62, or 46 miles (according to which channel is taken) above its mouth; up to Stockton, in seasons of high and medium water, there are three rivers, as it were, each of which is navigable by steam.

Fort Miller (map No. 1) is located on the unnavigable part of the river, 125 miles above Stockton. Tulare lake is regarded as the head of the river, though many small streams come down from the Sierra Nevada slope and join themselves as tributaries to it.

Of all the valleys of the Sierra Nevada slope, probably the Tulare valley is best adapted to the culture of the grape, and for this purpose not excelled by any known grape-growing region in the world.

At a considerable distance southeast of Tulare lake stands Fort Tejon, (map No. 1.) This fort commands the head of this valley, where there is an extensive Indian reservation. It occupies one of those important passes (spoken of in chapter II,) which, if well defended, would prevent the ingress of an invading force, landed on the southern coast of the department, into the heart of the State of California. It is in this respect that Fort Tejon, although now important in reference to Indians, may be of greater importance in future, and accordingly it should be kept up as a permanent post.

It will be seen that the Tulare and the Sacramento valleys, united, form a very extensive tract of country stretching far along the west slope of the Sierra Nevada range; constituting by its extent, its fertility, its settlements, the commerce on its rivers, its climate, its rich and inexhaustible gold mines, the great heart of our Pacific possessions.

The passes through the mountains at the southeastern extremity of this tract become the strategical points, which, with the Golden Gate, if well guarded, will insure permanent possession of this most valuable tract against any invading army that could be landed on our Pacific front.

Forts Miller and Reading derive their only importance from being in convenient positions, as temporary posts in the district, to keep order among the Indians and whites; and for a similar purpose a new dragoon post may be necessary in the Pit River valley, seen on map No. 1 coming down from the northeast of Fort Reading.

Between Fort Tejon and Fort Miller it is a good country for dragoons to operate in. It is a march of nine days for one company with its wagon train, and the distance is about 200 miles from fort to fort. From Fort Miller to Benicia barracks it is 187 miles, and a march of ten days for such a command. There is no difficulty from heaviness of roads on account of rains, between the middle of May and the first of December, for a body of dragoons to march from Fort Miller or Fort Reading to the new post recommended to be established in Pit River valley, keeping well in towards the foot hills of the Sierra Nevada. It is in this district of the department, after having the new post established, that the dragoons could be profitably employed by occasionally showing themselves to the Indians in that quarter.

IV.—*Military considerations in reference to the southeast part of the department of the Pacific.*

This chapter will contain the military topography of the department, east of the head of the Tulare valley and the Sierra Nevada range, to the Colorado river, and from the seacoast as far north as to include the sink of the Mohave river and the southern rim of the Great Basin.

Map No. 4 gives the country to the north, northeast, and northwest of the port of San Pedro, including the strategical pass as through the coast range of mountains, called the Sierra Madre, in the southern portion of the State of California.

Tejon is the name borne by the south part or extremity of the Tulare valley, referred to in the preceding chapter, and lies immediately at the base of the mountains where the Sierra Nevada and Sierra Madre come together. The Tejon is an excellent area of soil including the United States military reserve, selected for an Indian reservation in 1853. The place marked Depot Camp is a beautiful grove of oaks near a creek, and surrounded by an abundance of grass. It is in latitude 35° 2' 47" north, and longitude 118° 43' 31" west of Greenwich, and elevated 1,500 feet above the sea.

Passes in the Sierra Nevada.—1. *Cañada de las Uvas, (valley of the grape.)*—From the southern corner of the Tejon there is a gap in the mountains, running southeasterly, that is named Cañada de las Uvas Pass, through which there is a tolerable wagon road (for a mountain gorge) that may be taken in going to Los Angeles. This pass is said by Lieutenant Williamson, Corps Topographical Engineers, who surveyed it, "to run around the south end of the Sierra Nevada," and he treats it as dividing the Coast range, in the southern part of the State of California, from the Sierra Nevada range.

From its northern entrance we ascend a brook running into the Tejon and fed by springs situated about halfway up to the summit of the pass. In the vicinity of these springs is Fort Tejon. This post was established, by order of Major General Wool, commanding the department, in 1854, after approving the selection for the Indian reservation, whose shape and position are more clearly exhibited on map No. 6. The fort is somewhat to the south of the reserve, though within convenient distance of it, and it is undoubtedly the best position that could have been selected for the purposes intended by it. From the importance of this pass, in a military point of view, in regard to the Indians in the surrounding country, it is reasonable to infer that Fort Tejon will be kept up, notwithstanding the effects of an earthquake severely felt there last January, so severe as to injure the public buildings, and to drive the troops into the field for more safety than they could realize within doors. The shocks continued more or less violent for two to three days.

There is a wagon road from Fort Tejon to Fort Miller, the length of which is about 200 miles. From Fort Tejon, by the wagon road through the pass, *via* Lake Elizabeth, San Francisquito (Turner's) Pass, and San Fernando Misson, to Los Angeles, it is not far from 100 miles. A command of troops with its wagon train performed this march in 4 to 5 days in the summer of 1855.

2. *Tejon Pass.*—This runs from the northeastern angle of the said reserve through the Sierra Nevada; and there is a bad wagon road through it leading to the plain on the east side of the mountain range. From the reserve to the plain it is 18 miles; thence to Lake Elizabeth it is 24 miles, making the distance between the reserve and the lake 42 miles by this route.

3. *Ta-hic-ha-pa Pass* is about 6 miles north of the Tejon Pass, (see map No. 5,) and also leads through the Sierra Nevada range into the said plain; there is a wagon road through it; its summit is 4,020 feet above the sea, and lower than the summit of the Tejon Pass by 1,265 feet. The creek seen on the map bearing the same name, but sometimes called Walker's creek, is a tributary to Kern river.

At the head of the creek there is a beautiful prairie, 10 miles long by 4 wide, surrounded by high mountains. The waters from the east end of the prairie run into the Great Basin, so that the prairie is here the water shed of the Sierra Nevada. There were Indian rancherias in the prairie in 1853, when Lieutenant Williamson surveyed this pass, which he regards the least difficult of any in the Sierra Nevada through which to construct a railroad.

There certainly can be no very serious difficulty in constructing a good wagon road through it. In descending from the prairie, following the creek, (called Pass creek by Frémont,) the fall for $15\frac{1}{2}$ miles averages 157 feet per mile; the steepest grade is for $1\frac{1}{2}$ mile, at the rate of 192 feet per mile. Timber is abundant along the valley of this stream. On the east of the summit prairie, as we descend into the basin, for the first 6 miles the fall is less than 80 feet per mile, and further down the slope is more gradual. By passing from the prairie more directly by a southeasterly direction into the basin (as did Frémont) it is possible we might have a better route for a wagon road from the prairie towards the Mohave river.

4. *Walker's Pass* is, according to Lieutenant Williamson's recon-- naissance, 43 miles in a direction N. 30° E. from the prairie head-- waters of the Ta-hic-ha-pa. This places it 6 miles south of the 6th standard parallel south of Mt. Diablo, (map No. 5).

From Kern river, ascending the Chay-o-poo-ya-pah, it is 17 miles to the western extremity of the pass; thence to the summit it is 8 miles, where we are at an elevation of 5,300 feet above the sea; from the summit to the eastern extremity of the pass it is $8\frac{1}{4}$ miles.

Kern river is a bold, rapid stream, with steep banks and a narrow valley; it cañons 50 miles above Kern Lake. This lake is the head proper of the Tulare valley waters, and is only 400 feet above the level of the sea, and lower by 1,600 feet than the western extremity of Walker's Pass.

Gold mining on Kern river is successfully prosecuted; the quartz, in which it is found there, is of a friable nature, rendering it easy of pulverization; it contains some silver, which diminishes the value per ounce, but the ease with which the quartz is reduced to powder probably compensates for the presence of the less valuable metal.

The route via Kern river, the Chay-o-poo-ya pah creek, and Walker's Pass is a good one for connecting the Tulare valley by a wagon road with the Great Basin east of the Sierra Nevada range. The Kern river part would be expensive, owing to the cañon and the nearness of the spurs to the stream on either side in several places, but the grade on this part would not exceed 30 feet average per mile for 55 miles; in some places of this, however, the grade would exceed this average very considerably. On the Chay-o-poo-ya-pah they would not exceed 29 feet per mile anywhere. In the pass there would be only $1\frac{1}{2}$ mile where it would exceed 1 foot rise to one rod horizontal, in the steepest of which reach it is $1\frac{1}{3}$ foot rise to one rod horizontal, in the other parts of the pass it would not exceed 10 inches to the rod. The length of the route between Kern Lake and the east end of the pass is about 80 miles.

The valley of the Chay-o-poo-ya-pah is an Indian resort for gather- ing a sort of cane, upon the leaves of which is a kind of sugar, obtained by sun-drying and threshing the leaf. Good camping places for a company of dragoons are plenty in this valley.

H. Ex. Doc. 114——2

PASSES IN THE SIERRA MADRE.

1. *San Francisquito Pass* is now called Turner's Pass. Through it the roads from Cañada las Uvas, Tejon, and Ta-hic-ha-pa Passes all run to the Santa Clara valley, (map No. 4,) on the south side of the Sierra Madre (or Coast) range. In this (Turner's) pass "the road for many places is in the bed of a mountain stream through rocky cañons, and in several places at grades of 320 to 475 feet per mile."

2. *Soledad Pass.*—This was named by Lieut. Williamson, whose party surveyed it, "New Pass," and in his opinion it possesses less disadvantages than any other for running a railroad across this part of the Coast range. In ascending the pass from the rim of the Great Basin the steepest part is only one mile in extent, and the rate of ascent 218 to 240 feet per mile. The summit is 3,164 feet above the mean sea level. Descending towards the Pacific, in a reach of $5\frac{1}{2}$ miles, the grades do not exceed, in any place, 105 feet per mile. "There is no obstruction for a wagon except fallen trees. This pass leads into the Santa Clara valley near where the wagon road through the San Francisquito (Turner's) enters the same valley, from which point there is no obstruction to the ocean."

From these facts it would seem that for military purposes, requiring heavy wagon trains, New Pass would be better to improve for a military road from San Pedro to Fort Tejon than Turner's Pass, especially as the summit of the former is 272 feet lower than that of the latter.

3. *San Fernando Pass.*—On the south side of Santa Clara valley is a spur of the Coast range, called "Susannah," which is crossed through this pass in travelling between the valley and Los Angeles. The pass is 9 miles long, and its crest is 1,940 feet above the sea level. The road is difficult, though practicable for wagons through the pass. From San Fernando Mission the country may be traversed easily in almost any direction toward the coast and to San Bernardino.

As long as the military post, Fort Tejon, is kept up, the road from San Pedro via Los Angeles, through the "San Fernando Pass," thence across the Santa Clara, and up either the San Francisquito (Turner's) or up the Soledad (New) Pass, will have to be more or less used for military purposes; and there ought to be a liberal appropriation made out of the public treasury for improving all of these passes. The sum of $30,000 would be sufficient for the purpose. It is through this route that supplies reach Fort Tejon.

4. *Cajon Pass*, (map No. 4.)—In coming from "Depot Camp" on the Mohave, by the old Spanish trail, which is a good wagon road, the distance is 19 miles to the summit of this pass. The ascent from the north is easy. From the northern extremity of the pass to its summit it is $2\frac{1}{4}$ miles; thence descending southeasterly, following the Cajon creek, it is steep for $1\frac{1}{4}$ mile; thence for $6\frac{1}{4}$ miles it is easier, the grade being 200 feet per mile; thence for the next $6\frac{1}{2}$ miles 100 feet per mile. The whole distance from the summit to the southern extremity of the pass is 14 miles, and from this extremity to San Bernardino it is 14 miles—making the distance between the Mohave

and this town, 47 miles, which, for a mountain pass, having its summit 4,676 feet above the level of the sea, is a tolerable wagon road.

Sycamore Grove is on this route, near the mouth of Cajon Creek. It is here that General P. Smith, United States army, thought of establishing a post, when in command of this department. Lieut. Mowry's detachment, after marching from Salt Lake valley, encamped here for one week. I doubt not it would be found well suited for a post, should one be needed in this district. It would be supplied through the port of San Pedro with all such necessary articles as are not produced in that region.

5. *San Gorgonia Pass*, (see maps 4 and 6.)—Mount San Bernardino is said to be the highest peak in the range, and 9,000 feet above the sea. Southwest, at a distance of 30 miles, is the peak San Jacinto, nearly as high. Between their bases lies the Gorgonia Pass—one of the lowest in the coast range—being at its summit 2,800 feet above the sea. The grades in this are easy, and there is no great difficulty in passing a wagon train through it. From San Bernardino to the summit of the pass it is 27 miles; thence to its eastern extremity $18\frac{1}{3}$ miles; thence to Fort Yuma on the Colorado, in a straight line across the desert bearing N. 85° E., the distance is 130 miles.

NORTH OF THE COAST RANGE.

Mohave river, (map No. 4.)—I shall here give results of the exploration of this water-course, by Lieuts. Williamson and Parke, Corps Topographical Engineers, in October and November, 1853, and other results corroborative, which I have obtained from notes of the land surveyors kindly furnished me at the United States surveyor general's office in San Francisco. It is from these notes that I have constructed maps 5 and 6, and filled them with all the topography obtained up to the beginning of the surveying season of 1857. It will be seen that I have given the whole of the Mohave and its sink, also a definite position of a part of the hitherto unexplored Colorado above Fort Yuma.

The Mohave takes its rise in the northern slopes of the San Bernardino mountains. The country near its source is so rugged as to render travelling there upon mule back very difficult, and often impossible. It is impossible to cross the mountains here with wagons.

At "Depot Camp," marked on the map, the river is broad and shallow in autumn. Its banks here are well wooded, and its bottom is confined between terraces on either side, from one to three miles apart; as we descend from here the water, however, soon sinks in the sandy bed, reappearing generally at a point of rocks, or where a contraction occurs. Timber exists in places along the direction of the river, but generally disappears with the water. About 30 miles below Depot Camp it appears at a point of rocks and flows freely, but only for a short distance. From here, following a broad river bed for 35 miles, "we come to a cañon about 7 miles long, having running water through its whole extent. In this cañon the bed of the river is from 100 to 150 feet wide, and on either side the clay bluffs rise over 100 feet in height vertically. These banks present the appearance of gothic pillars, and the clay of which they are composed is of every variety of tint—purple, pink, blue, yellow, &c. In the cañon cane was growing, and large quantities had been cut by the Indians.''

''On emerging from the cañon a sandy plain is met, and all signs of the river bed are lost. It is 13 miles across this plain; upon it there is an abundant growth of mezquite trees, and some old abandoned Indian huts. To the north of this plain there is a salt lake bed, on the edge of which, at the base of the hills, there are several fine springs, slightly brackish, but not unpalatable; around there was good grass in November. Further to the north there is another salt lake bed of hard clay bottom. The two are from 3 to 4 miles apart, connected by a ditch 20 feet wide and 2 feet deep.''

Lieut. Williamson concludes the first of these lake beds to be the true sink of the Mohave river, and his reasons for the opinion are founded upon his own observations.

From the Depot Camp, I find by the plots of the land surveys, the distance is 90 miles to the border of the lake bed that is regarded as the sink. The bearing of the sink from the camp is N. 63° E., and the shortest distance from the sink to the Colorado, into which it was formerly supposed the Mohave ran, is about 66 miles.

From Depot Camp to the Mohave Indian settlement on the left bank of the Colorado, 6 miles above the entrance of Williams' branch, it is about 156 miles, and the direction is N. 83° E. Following this direction we should come to the south base of Providence mountains, where there are several springs, at a distance from the camp on the Mohave of about 80 miles.

This same direction would leave a volcano to the north, situated about 15 miles from Depot Camp in a direct line to the sink. And it would pass over rough mountains and between two old craters, which are about 54 miles from said camp.

I have been somewhat particular in describing these landmarks, so that in case of a necessity of troops being ordered into this district between the Mohave and Colorado, they may easily find their way over this desolate region.

Of the Great Basin, maps 4, 5, 6, show the rim, as it were, of that portion immediately north of the Coast range, and east of the southern extremity of the Sierra Nevada, as far as the Colorado. From the base of the Coast range northward there is a belt of undulating land, 15 to 20 miles in width, and unbroken by peaks. This belt stretches, as seen on map 4, for nearly 100 miles to the headwaters of the Mohave. From the eastern extremity of Tejon Pass, in a direction following the bases of Lost Hills, for 30 miles there are several springs to be met, from which issue little streams, sinking, however, in the dry soil after running a few yards. In coming westward from the Mohave, on the route seen dotted on map 4, Lieut. Williamson found no water. ''Independent of the Lost Hills, the country is a system of inclined planes, in which the grades often approach 100 feet per mile. There is no timber; the surface is generally bare, or covered with sage bushes, greasewood, yuca trees,'' &c.

In proceeding from Lake Elizabeth with a wagon train along the north base of the Coast range, by keeping close in by the foot hills water and grass may be had at convenient distances, for camping a marching command of one company of dragoons, and perhaps two. There are several springs on the route, and a bold stream (Johnson's river) emerges from the hills, but immediately sinks on reaching the rim of the basin. From this river to the Spanish trail the country is filled with yuca trees and bushes. In October, 1853, Lieut. Stoneman conducted the wagon train of Lieut. Williamson's party over this route from the Tejon, through the Cañada de las Uvas Pass, without much difficulty, to the Mohave river

In the part of the basin immediately north of the belt aforesaid "is a system of isolated peaks and short ridges, known as Lost mountains, and which, as they extend north and increase in height, become worthy of the name of mountain ranges. These often enclose extensive areas which are destitute of peaks, and in the lowest part, where water accumulates after heavy rains, is a lake bed without water in a dry season."

Therefore, were an expedition undertaken, with an object requiring a march into or leading through this extensive region, at the time of a dry season, difficulties of no small magnitude, in respect to obtaining a sufficiency of water and grass, might be encountered by the command.

SOUTH OF THE COAST RANGE.

From map 4 it might possibly be inferred that the southern slope of the Coast range in this district is beautifully and abundantly watered at all seasons throughout the whole country; nothing would be more erroneous than such an idea. The numerous dark lines shown on the map as so many head branches of the Santa Clara, the San Gabriel, the Los Angeles, and the Santa Anna, only indicate the natural drains from the mountain gorges and ravines in times of an abundance of rain. In the dry seasons very many of these have not a drop of water in them. Nevertheless, this district is a fertile country, abounding in grapes and other fruit, good pasturage and grain. The towns and villages are small. There are, however, a goodly number of settlements scattered over the country; it has several old missions, also several large valuable ranches. San Bernardino is settled principally by Mormons.

Table of distances.

Distances from—	To—	Miles.
Fort Tejon *via* Turner's Pass	San Bernardino	155
Fort Tejon *via* New Pass	San Bernardino	179
Fort Tejon *via* Cajon Pass	San Bernardino	121
Fort Tejon	Depot Camp, Mohave	107
Depot Camp	San Bernardino	47
Depot Camp	Seven-mile Cañon, Mohave	65
Depot Camp, (direct line)	Colorado	156
Depot Camp, (direct line)	Sink of Mohave	90
San Bernardino	East extremity Gorgonia Pass	43
East extremity San Gorgonia Pass	Fort Yuma, (direct line)	130
San Bernardino	Los Angeles	56
Los Angeles	San Pedro	25
Depot Camp, Mohave	North entrance New Pass	55
North entrance New Pass	Summit New Pass	3
Summit New Pass	East fork Santa Clara river	22
East fork Santa Clara river	Entrance San Fernando Pass	4
Entrance Pass	Summit of Pass	4
Summit of Pass	Mission of San Fernando	6
Mission San Fernando	Cabuang Ranch	11
Cabuang Ranch	Los Angeles	10
Los Angeles	Mission San Gabriel	9
Mission San Gabriel	San Gabriel, (creek crossing)	7
Crossing San Gabriel creek	Qui Qual Mango Ranch	26
Qui Qual Mango Ranch	Sycamore Grove	14
Sycamore Grove	San Bernardino	3
Fort Tejon *via* Turner's Pass	San Pedro *via* Los Angeles	125
San Pedro	San Francisco, by sea	320
San Pedro	San Francisco, by land	434
San Pedro	San Diego, by land	97
Los Angeles	San Diego	103

EAST OF SAN DIEGO TO FORT YUMA.

This portion, which is the southernmost port of the military department of the Pacific, is, as much as we have occasion for, seen on map 7.)

I have already spoken, in chapter II, of San Diego being in possession of a good natural harbor for commercial and, by consequence, for military purposes, in their relations with the southern part of the department.

There is no navigation in the San Diego river; all that the government expended here for the improvement of the mouth of the river seems to have been little better than thrown away, from not following up the first appropriation with another sufficient to bring the work to a condition of security against the next year's freshet.

This is the port at which troops from San Francisco, or other ports north, are landed, to march thence either to Fort Yuma or to other points, as needed in the extreme southern portion of the department. We now have troops of the 1st dragoons and the headquarters of the regiment at the Mission of San Diego. It has been (until quite recently) a one company artillery post for ten years past.

The field of the battle of San Pasqual, of the 6th and 7th of December, 1846, is marked on the map. It was here that our troops, under Colonel Kearney, and the Californians, under General Pico, had their obstinate contest for two days before the latter were forced to quit the field.

From San Diego there is a tolerably good road running directly down into Lower California of Mexico; also from here there is a passable road for wagons *via* San Pasqual, San Felipe, &c., to Fort Yuma; also a pack trail leading more directly over the mountains. It is the wagon route to Fort Yuma that will be more fully described, as it is the route the troops are obliged to follow.

From San Diego to San Pasqual, 39 miles, and thence 12 miles to Santa Marie, the road is good for wagon trains, and the grazing and water on this reach of 51 miles are good the year round. At Santa Marie the pack trail from San Diego comes in, shortening the distance 14 miles. From San Pasqual valley the road crosses a spur, which it is impossible to avoid, so steep for four miles that a team can only haul half the load with which it started from San Diego.

From Santa Marie to San Felipe ranch it is 43 miles. On this reach grass and water are plenty, and grass for 8 miles further. At Santa Isabel, 15 miles from Santa Marie, the pack trail leaves the wagon road and passes to the right; from 8 miles beyond San Felipe to the Jornada there is little, if any, grazing, and no water. Immediately on leaving the Indian hut at San Felipe we are on the desert. Forage must be taken for the animals in crossing this desert.

From San Felipe to Vallecito it is 18 miles, and water is found 13 miles from San Felipe, or 5 miles before coming to Vallecito; thence to Coresito (cane) creek 18 miles. The road is very heavy, it being sandy. The water of Cane creek sometimes poisons animals. From Cane creek to Sackett's Wells it is 21 miles; thence to Big Laguna, on or near New river, 10 miles; thence down the bed of this river for 10 miles to "Camp Salvation." It was here that the immigrants of 1849 met the river coming up; this was a flow caused by the freshet of the Colorado for the first time in ten years; a most fortunate circumstance for those people, who had been 50 hours from any water. We thus make the reach from San Felipe to Camp Salvation, on New river, 77 miles by the road.

On leaving New river the next point of importance to be reached by the traveller is Alamo Muchos, 12 miles. Here there are wells affording water to man and beast. From the Alamo Wells to Indian or Cook's Wells it is 30 miles. The road is level and of heavy sand on this reach of 42 miles. From Cook's Wells to the Colorado it is 16 miles, and the road is good, coming out on the river at Algodones, 15 miles below the junction of the Gila and Colorado. Fort Yuma is at this junction, on the right bank of the Colorado. We thus make the road 244 miles long between San Diego and Fort Yuma. A portion of the road, as seen on the map, is within Mexican territory.

It takes 7 days to make the journey by a wagon conveyance, and 5 days on horseback by the pack trail. The desert is sometimes covered with water from rain. The soil is so compact as to hold water for some time.

The march between San Diego and Fort Yuma is exceedingly laborious and difficult for troops to perform, still it has been successfully accomplished several times. Brevet Major Reynolds, of the 3d artillery, marched his company across, most successfully, in the month of August, 1855, without the loss of a man or animal, in 10 days.

Colorado river, emptying into the Gulf of California, divides the Mexican from the United States possessions up to a point 50 to 60 miles north of its mouth, above that it is wholly within the United States territory. It is successfully navigated by steamers of very light draught up to Fort Yuma, by the river windings, 125 miles above its mouth. The Gila is said by some to be navigable in high stages for some distance, but little or no dependence can be placed on its navigability at any time. In relation to the Colorado below Fort Yuma, I quote from the report of Lieutenant Derby, Corps Topographical Engineers, who says: "It has a strong current, and the channel is somewhat obstructed with snags, and is narrow, and the frequent shifting of the sandy bed makes the navigation quite intricate. The action of the tide ceases at about 40 miles above its mouth. It is impossible to sail up the river above that point.. At its mouth there is a depth of two fathoms of water."

There are now no towns or settlements of any importance on the lower Colorado, and the valley is forbidding in the extreme.

The whole course of the river from Fort Yuma to the Gulf may be said to be through an exceedingly uninteresting desert. The climate of the valley is well calculated to enervate human energy. The extremes of temperature are such as to show the maximum to be 116 degrees F., and the minimum 36 degrees, at Fort Yuma during the year; and the annual fall of rain amounts to only $1\frac{3}{4}$ inches. The heat of the summer is such as to preclude bodily exertion in the open air, nevertheless the troops are generally very healthy, and the post is undoubtedly in the very best position that could have been found, and its importance is being more and more appreciated every day. The new mail route between San Antonio, Texas, and San Diego, California, passes by Fort Yuma. The first mail was recently carried through in 34 days from San Antonio to San Diego.

Fort Yuma is supplied from Benicia depot by means of a government sail vessel, as far as to the head of the Gulf of California, thence by steamboats, of which there are two plying on the lower Colorado, and owned by individuals. These boats do all the transportation on the river.

The trip of the sail vessel from Benicia, out and back, generally consumes three to four months. The voyage is necessarily long. The shortest steamer run from Benicia to the mouth of the Colorado is 2.110 miles; this furnishes some idea of the distance a sail vessel would run to perform the trip. From our military post, San Diego, to Fort Yuma, the steamer run by sea is 1,625 miles to the mouth of the Colorado; thence by river 125 miles—in all, 1,750 miles. The overland wagon road distance between the same posts, as before said, is 244 miles.

In a late report from an officer of high rank and commanding position, in referring to the desert and the difficulties in the way of supplying Fort Yuma, he forcibly and truly remarks: "The route to Fort Yuma is by land in part, and by water entirely, within the territory of Mexico." He propounds the question: "Would it not be sound policy to submerge the desert from the Colorado and convert thus a barren waste into a navigable lake?"

Did this question not emanate from one high in position, and, by consequence, one whose opinion might be supposed to carry weight even to conviction, I would not notice it here, by affirming that such a project is practically impossible to execute, even admitting the data to be true upon which he bases the idea of converting the desert into a smiling lake of navigable water.

The Colorado above Fort Yuma is very imperfectly known, except the small portion shown on my map, No. 6 It has never been explored with a view to develop its capacity for navigation or adaptation for the abode of civilization. Should it prove susceptible of steam navigation, even though it be no better than the lower part of the river, it will become highly advantageous for carrying on military operations in the department of the Pacific, in so far as they may have relation to Utah.

The stories of some old trappers and Indians, who presume to be familiar with the upper Colorado, would almost make us believe that its banks in certain places are gilt with gold, and at others paved with copper, iron, and even silver and precious stones. The exploration lately ordered by the Hon. Secretary of War, it is to be hoped, will solve the several interesting problems connected with this river.

V.—*Military considerations in reference to tl : Utah portion of the department of the Pacific.*

Map No. 8 represents as much of the Territory of Utah as is necessary to be referred to in order fully to comprehend its military connexion with the other portions of this department.

There are three prominent routes, marked in red on the map, connecting Utah with the other parts of the department, viz: with the southern part of the State of California, the middle part of that State, and the Territory of Oregon.

Southern route.—This may be regarded as starting from the port of San Pedro, (see map No. 4,) and passing through Los Angeles, the Cajon Pass, in the Coast range, to the Mohave river. This reach of 110 miles, from San Pedro to the river, has been sufficiently described in chapter IV. Again, from Fort Tejon, a command could start and pass through the Cañada de las Uvas, as also mentioned in that chapter, and follow along by the foot-hills of the north slope of the coast range, and intersect the road from San Pedro at the Mohave. This route from Fort Tejon is indicated on maps Nos. 4 and 5, and the length of the route is 107 miles.

From this intersection, which may be regarded as at Depot Camp, on the Mohave, the road follows generally the right bank of the river for a distance of 48 miles, where it crosses to the left bank, and up to this point on the route no difficulty opposes itself to the movement of any command with its wagon train, however large. Grass and water are good and abundant in the valley of the Mohave, and there is wood on its banks at most of the places where the river remains above ground.

On leaving the Mohave the country becomes almost a desert. From this river to Bitter Spring, 44 miles; thence, by way of Resting Spring, 91 miles, to Las Vegas, (the plains,) the road is difficult, water not good, grass poor, and it would be a serious undertaking to march a large command over it, though by great care it could be successfully accomplished.

From Bitter Spring all the way to Pure Water Spring, on the Amagosia, there is little or no grass or water. The Amagosia is a putrid stream, running through a deep cañon, along whose sides it is difficult to pass. It was within about 14 miles of Pure Water Spring that Mr. Soublettes party obtained gold with success in 1850, 1851, and 1852, packing the water for washing it from that spring, until driven off after several were killed by Indians. In descending to the Vegas the road passes through a cañon, affording excellent cover for an attacking party of Indians.

The Vegas is a small stream of good water, but it sinks; it heads in a spring that boils with such force that a person cannot sink in it. Along the course of the stream grass is good and abundant, and it affords the only really good camping place after leaving the Mohave. It is understood that there is a settlement of Mormons at Las Vegas. It is supposed the Colorado river comes within 25 miles of this settlement. Should it prove navigable for light draught steamers up to the entrance of Virgin river, this point becomes important in reference to a new communication from southern California into Utah, *via* the Colorado river.

From the Vegas to Muddy river, 43 miles, the road is good, but there is little or no water. Lieut. Mowry's detachment made this march in 18 hours, using the night, halting to refresh the animals on an intervening patch of grass.

From Muddy river the road is descending for 20 miles, when it comes to Virgin river; from here it ascends the valley of the latter for about 23 miles, thence about 19 miles to the Santa Clara river; from this it follows up the valley of this stream for about 27 miles, and then we soon come to Mountain Meadows. On this reach of 89 miles, between the Muddy and the Meadows, there is no serious difficulty in the way of a wagon train. The road along the Virgin crosses the stream often, and is trying to the animals; in some places the bottom is of shifting sand. The crossings of the Santa Clara are frequent, but they are narrow and easy to be made. "The cañon through which it flows is susceptible of a strong defence by a small body, which, if properly posted, could stop or annoy a much larger force."

Mountain Meadows—425 miles from San Pedro, 315 miles from where the road leaves the Mohave, 318 miles from Fort Tejon—is a beautiful plateau, seven to eight thousand feet above the level of the ocean; it is shut in by the mountains, grows luxurious grass of an excellent quality for grazing, and is intersected by a never-failing stream of pure cold water. Lieut. Mowry says "it is one of the few places on the route the traveller remembers with pleasure." He regards the mountains here as the southern rim of the Salt Lake Basin. It is apparent to me that these meadows would afford a good military position for commanding the whole route hence to Salt Lake City.

From Mountain Meadows to Cedar City it is about 35 miles, and probably it is about the same distance to Harmony, and the road is descending. "These two towns are inhabited by miners and iron-workers, and several large furnaces are in active operation, affording employment for several thousand men. The ore is of the richest quality and the supply inexhaustible. Highly ornamented castings are produced, and the manufacture of cannon is said to be in successful operation."

The respective distances from Cedar City to Parowan City; thence to Fillmore, the capital of Utah; thence to Salt Lake City, as recorded in Lieut. Mowry's report, are different from those given on the map. He gives them 20, 90, 150 miles; whereas the map gives them 39, 55, 128 miles; here are great discrepancies. On the whole extent, however, between Cedar City and Salt Lake City, the road is excellent, and water occurs all the way at convenient distances; but fuel is scarce, though attainable at some inconvenience. The country is well settled by Mormons, and villages and small towns occur frequently, outwardly evincing thrift and quietude.

It will be seen that I make the approximate total distance, estimating by the map, from San Pedro to Great Salt Lake City 682 miles. It would be a march of about 40 marching days. From San Pedro to Mountain Meadows, where the command would be placed beyond all difficulties, it would be a march of 22 to 25 days.

The detachment under Lieut. Mowry made the march from United States Camp, in Rush valley, 45 miles southwest of Salt Lake City, to Fort Tejon, in the summer of 1855, at the rate of 26 miles per day, according to his estimate of the total distance; and he says "several marches of 30 miles and more per day were without water and temperature at 120 F."

He reports, that "with care in husbanding the strength of the animals before reaching the desert, and attention to them while crossing it, the march could be made without material loss. Two artesian wells on the desert, that is, between the Mohave and Las Vegas, and one between the Vegas and Muddy rivers, would make the route easy for travel at all seasons. The proper time for starting would be from 1st to 15th April, or 1st September. In the autumn the deserts are covered with water from rains and there is a second crop of grass. The route is healthy at all seasons."

INDIANS.

On the Vegas, the Virgin, the Muddy, and the Santa Clara, there are hundreds of Indian warriors, who Lieut. Mowry reports "have been taught to believe the Mormon people to be altogether superior to the Americans—morally, mentally, and physically. In each tribe two or more Mormon missionaries were found, whose object was to impress upon the Indians the belief in the inferiority and hostility of the Americans, and the superiority and friendship of the Mormons. And Brigham Young counsels his people to intermarry with the Indians.''

''There are many places well known to the Indians on this route easily defensible against a large force.''

A company of dragoons might leave Fort Tejon or San Pedro, make an easy march through these tribes, and return in three months; the beneficial effect of which cannot be doubted. If from Fort Tejon, the march should be direct to the Mohave, following the foot-hills of the north slope of the Coast range.

Ascending the Colorado to Utah.—We have seen how difficult the land march is from the Mohave to Las Vegas, a distance of 135 miles, across a portion that may be regarded almost a desert. If the Colorado, as is supposed it does, comes to within 25 miles of Las Vegas, and prove navigable for small steamers up to the junction of the Virgin, it will be fortunate, for it will be seen, should all this be true, we should have land carriage of only about 40 to 50 miles up the valley of the Virgin to the point where the present road strikes this stream; and from the junction to Mountain Meadows it would be only 109 miles.

If, while the troops are in Utah, a military reconnaissance could be made from Cedar City, *via* Mountain Meadows, down the Virgin river to the Colorado, to test the practicability of opening a road, the results would b. valuable to the War Department. I doubt if there would be more than 50 miles in extent of country to examine, and it would all be within 144 miles of Cedar City. While at the junction the character of the Colorado for some few miles above and below should be ascertained in reference to its capacity for navigation.

Middle route, or route from the valley of the Sacramento to Utah.— Should it become necessary to march a command from this valley into Utah it would be best to organize it to start its land march from the city of Sacramento.

From Sacramento to Placerville it is 25 miles; thence to the west foot of the pass in the Sierra Nevada, seen on the map to the south of Lake Bigler, it is about 30 miles; thence fairly through the pass to its eastern extremity, about 10 miles. This pass is by way of one of the head branches of the American river. In this reach of 80 miles the only temporary difficulty to be encountered, starting as early as the middle of May, would probably be snow in the pass. The condition of the snow, however, could always be learned beforehand at Placerville, and the time of commencing the march regulated accordingly. In this pass there are more permanent difficulties than snow—steepness of grades and rocky places; but, notwithstanding these, wagon trains pass through it without serious detention.

From the east extremity of the pass to Reese, where the road comes to near Carson river, it is about 25 miles. Carson valley is a noted district on this route, affording good soil, water, and grass in abundance, and it will afford a good position in Utah for a military post when needed; and it would be well for the War Department to make a reservation, the sooner the better, for the purpose. Carson river is said to sink, or to be lost in the earth, in its course running eastward.

From Carson river to Ragtown it is about 25 miles; thence to the southeast point of Lake Humboldt it is 35 miles; and in this latter portion there is a desert to cross, where, however, no serious difficulty would be encountered.

From the said point of the lake to Lawson's Meadows it is about 45 miles.

I thus make the total distance between the city of Sacramento and Lawson's Meadows 210 miles. Two companies of Brevet Lieutenant Colonel Steptoe's command, with their wagon train complete, marched by this route, though in an opposite direction, from the Meadows to the city, between the 14th June and 9th July, 1855—26 days. Of course the greatest obstacles to the movement of the train were met in the crossing of the Nevada ridge.

Lawson's Meadows are near where the Humboldt river, after pursuing a course bearing a little south of west for about $3\frac{1}{4}$ degrees in longitude, suddenly turns to the south, and then, after showing itself for an extent of about one-half a degree in latitude, is lost in its sink, which is Lake Humboldt. These meadows undoubtedly present an important position for military purposes. It is here that a concentration of troops could be effected, one body starting from Fort Lane Oregon, the other from Sacramento, or indeed from any point in the valley of the Sacramento river. It is a position pretty well east of the Sierra Nevada range and well into Utah. It is believed it possesses all the requirements for a military reservation. It is somewhere not far south of here that the United States wagon road, appropriated so liberally for by Congress last year, will run across Utah to Honey Lake, California; and it is somewhere near these meadows that another wagon road may be expected to diverge to reach the Willamette river valley in Oregon.

From Lawson's Meadows, proceeding further into Utah, the route is up the narrow valley of the Humboldt river for an extent of about 175 miles. This valley may be safely marched through any time in the summer after the 10th of June, when the grass will be abundant, the road and the water good. But before that time the river is alkaline and the grass covered with water; the valley being narrow the track will be over abrupt knolls, difficult for the passage of a train.

It is a march of 13 days between Lawson's Meadows and the last crossing seen on the map in ascending the Humboldt.

From that crossing by the north and east of Great Salt Lake to the City of Salt Lake—the largest Mormon town—the distance is estimated at 210 miles. The roads on this part of the route are good by the 1st of May and afterwards, and grass plenty except in Goose Creek mountains. The march from the meadows to this town would occupy the command about 30 days.

I make the total length from Sacramento City to Salt Lake City 595 miles. Whatever may be the error in the distance here given, Steptoe's command made the march in an opposite direction between April 28 and July 9, 1855.

It is quite probable the route we are considering is the best, under all circumstances affecting the case, for a wagon road from Sacramento City to intersect the one before mentioned across Utah to Honey Lake valley. Here we perceive another fact of importance connected with Lawson's Meadows—as it must be somewhere in their vicinity that a road will diverge from the United States trunk road across Utah in a southwest direction, to reach the permanent head of navigation on the Sacramento river.

ROUTE FROM OREGON TO UTAH.

Should the object be to march a command, drawn from the troops located in Oregon, into Utah it would be best to assemble them at Fort Lane, Oregon Territory, which is on Rogue river, (see map No. 9,) as through the Willamette valley, they could be assembled from the Columbia river posts, and from the Puget Sound district—and all concentrated at Fort Lane in time to commence the march by June 10. This arrangement would enable the quartermaster's department to take advantage of the favorable stage of water for transportation up the Willamette river to the head of its navigation, and of the favorable condition of the roads thence to Fort Lane.

From Fort Lane to the west foot of Applegate Pass, of the Cascade range, 27 miles, there is little or no difficulty in the way of a wagon train.

From the west to east foot of the pass it is probably 10 miles, which will bring us to Klamath river; through the pass there is no serious obstacle to the passage of a train of wagons.

From Klamath river to the southeast end of Rhett lake it is about 17 miles; from here to the stream supplying Clear lake it is 10 miles; from this to Ingalls' lake it is 10 miles. In this reach from Klamath river to Ingalls' lake, 52 miles, the road has water and grass in abundance, and there is no serious impediment. Ingalls' lake is the first or left-hand one seen on map 8, nearly up to the boundary line between California and Oregon. Klamath and Rhett are not on this map.

From Ingalls' lake to the outlet of Goose lake, supposed to be Pit river, it is about 55 miles, and until we get within 8 miles of the south end of the lake the road is bad. The first part is through low and muddy spots, and then we come to a rocky ridge or divide 12 miles over, upon which the stones, though not large, would be severe upon the feet of the animals. The bend over the ridge might be shortened, probably, by opening a road to the south of the present one.

Goose lake is a fine sheet of good fresh water, it being the receptacle of many cool mountain brooks. The lake is 25 to 30 miles long by 10 wide, and around its shores and in the narrow ravines of the brooks there is an abundance of grass for almost any number of animals at the proper season. It is in the vicinity of this lake that Brevet Captain Warner, Topographical Engineers, and his party were massacred while engaged in a topographical exploration of this region.

From the outlet of Goose lake to the summit of the Sierra Nevada it is probably about 15 miles. The pass of the mountain here is by no means a difficult one, and its extent is only about 8 to 10 miles.

The east slope is rather steep, but comparatively free from rocks; the lake immediately on the east of it is of bad water. Captain Ingalls is of the opinion, from his observation, that by considerable labor in opening a road through the heavy timber further south some distance could be saved and the grade rendered easier than on the present track. On June 23, 1855, the day he crossed, there was no snow in the pass.

From the east foot of the pass to the great cañon it is about 45 miles, and the road is tolerably good. Through the cañon it is estimated to be 25 miles, and, though somewhat tedious, the road is passable for a train, or can be rendered so by some little attention to the bad spots.

From the southern extremity of the cañon to Black Rock it is about 25 miles. On this reach, and for a distance of about 35 miles further the country in summer is a sterile dry waste. It may be called a desert, of about 60 miles across, in which water and grass of good quality are not met with, and it is on this part of the route that extra care should be taken to insure the successful passage of a train. There are some boiling springs and a slough with alkaline water. "It is decidedly dangerous to permit stock to more than taste it." Late in the season the condition of the water and grass is at its worst, and it would then be a dangerous experiment for all the animals of a large train to attempt to cross it. In early spring the desert is so much covered with water as not to be passable without great difficulty.

From the southern point of the desert to Lawson's Meadows it is 18 miles. In this part of the route the road is good, and water and grass of excellent quality exist in abundance.

I make the total distance on this route from Fort Lane to Lawson's Meadows 315 miles. Captain Ingalls estimated it at 368 miles. His detachment was 23 days marching it, though in an opposite direction, and consisted of 122 horses, 112 mules, 17 wagons, and 50 dragoons. The march was made between June 14 and July 6, 1855. The captain says "between Fort Lane and the desert the grass and water were abundant and a more interesting country at that season I never saw."

I have already spoken of the importance of Lawson's Meadows, and of the probability of a wagon road diverging in this neighborhood, from the United States road across Utah to Honey Lake, to reach the Willamette valley in Oregon. It is highly probable the route I have just been describing is the best that can be followed for this purpose. The desert is the only objection to it; and, notwithstanding this, it is doubtful if any route except this can be found for feasible communication between the settled parts of Oregon and Washington Territories.

From Lawson's Meadows the route would be common with that already described, being up the Humboldt river, as a part of the route from Sacramento City to Salt Lake City, if the command were destined around by the north and east of Salt Lake to the great Mormon city.

From Fort Lane, Oregon Territory, to Great Salt Lake City, I make the total distance 700 miles on this route, and it would require 66 days for a command of four to five companies to accomplish the march.

Manner of sending troops into Utah.—Hitherto all that have been sent into and through this Territory have been assembled, from the departments of the east and west, at Fort Leavenworth, on the Missouri, and began their march from that post. Prior to the present year two marches of this kind have been executed: one by the rifle regiment in 1849, the other by a command under Brevet Lieutenant Colonel Steptoe in 1854–'55. The route of the former diverged at Green river to the northward, and entered Oregon by the way of Fort Hall and the Snake river; that of the latter was from Fort Leavenworth, 311 miles, 21 days, to Fort Kearney; thence, 336 miles, 23 days, to Fort Laramie; thence, 290 miles, 24 days, to Pacific springs, the west extremity of South Pass of Rocky mountains; and thence, 232 miles, 20 days, to Great Salt Lake City. The command left Fort Leavenworth June 1 and arrived at Salt Lake City August 31, 1854. It is believed that the stoppages were no more than necessary to accomplish this march of 1,169 miles in 92 days, without breaking down men and animals, and that this is a pretty fair measure of the minimum time in practice that it would be proper to spend on so long a march over a similar country by a body of troops of a respectable number. It seems that the actual number of marching days was 64, making the average distance per marching day a little more than 18 miles; or, if we include the stoppages to rest, $12\frac{2}{3}$ miles per day from the beginning to the end of the march.

Now, this rate of marching, which was in the department of the west, being applied to the department of the Pacific will give us the times for the marches, including stoppages to rest the command, as follows:

From Sacramento to Salt Lake City, 47 days.

From San Pedro to Salt Lake City, 54 days.

It takes 25 days to transport a regiment by steam from New York, and 22 from New Orleans, *via* Panama, to San Francisco, thence one day to Sacramento and two to San Pedro, including all necessary delays for transhipment; and it is obvious the regiment could be assembled from various posts in or east of the valley of the Mississippi at New York or New Orleans quite as expeditiously as at Fort Leavenworth.

Hence, if it be an object with the War Department to despatch troops in the least possible time—from posts so located, regardless of other considerations—to Salt Lake City, the quickest way is to assemble them either at New York or New Orleans, and embark them by steam for San Francisco, thence to Sacramento, and from there march them to Salt Lake City.

If embarked from New York the saving would be 19 days, if New Orleans 22 days, in the time that would be consumed in marching them from Fort Leavenworth to the same point. If sent by steam from San Francisco to San Pedro, and marched thence to Salt Lake City, the saving would be 11 or 14 days in the time required to march them from Fort Leavenworth.

VI.—*Military considerations in reference to the Oregon portion of the department of the Pacific.*

Southern Oregon, so much as to include the southwest portion, is represented on map No. 9. The boundary between the State of California and the Territory of Oregon is the 42d parallel of north latitude. The town of Crescent City is in California, about 13 miles south of the boundary. After passing Humboldt bay this is the next port possessing any military importance north of San Francisco, from which, by the steamer's track, it is distant about 320 miles. It can be safely entered at all times, except in fogs and during the prevalence of south and east winds; but there being no piers or docks lighterage has to be resorted to.

It was through Crescent City that Fort Lane, while garrisoned, was supplied. The fort is 85 to 100 miles distant from it in the interior, following the pack trail, seen on the map, which runs through an exceedingly broken country. It was Crescent City that General Wool selected to be made the principal centre of operations of the troops for closing the Indian war in southern Oregon in 1856. The results showed the wisdom of the selection.

With the exception of the Coquille and the Umpqua the rivers represented on map No. 9 are not at all navigable except for canoes, being generally of rapid current, rocky beds, and in many places running through deep cañons.

Rogue river, named ''Trashit'' in the aboriginal tongue, was by legislative enactment changed in name to '' Gold river;'' but from causes which I omit to mention, all persons outside of the valley of this stream still persist in the use of the first appellative. This river, coming from the west slope of the Cascade range, is of rapid current, and only navigable even for canoes in a few of its reaches. Its lower half is full of rapids and cañons. It has no considerable valley until we get some 40 to 60 miles above its mouth; and then we come to a beautiful and fertile one, of only about 30 miles in extent, however; it is this that is called the Rogue River valley, in which is situated Fort Lane. Great difficulties are in the way of opening a road or passing from the mouth of the river up to this valley; the trails are circuitous, tortuous, rough, and steep; and it is only under difficulties that this tempting and much coveted valley can be reached from any point on the coast.

Coos bay is important in respect to its coal veins. Small vessels enter it to receive the coal which, being of a quality valuable for domestic purposes, is mined in considerable quantities; but as yet it is not profitable for sea steamer purposes, requiring too much bulk for a given amount of heat—two to three bushels of this giving only the heat of one of anthracite. As the veins are more deeply penetrated, however, the coal is found to improve in quality.

It is but a mere step, as it were, from Coos bay across to the Coquille river; and it is quite probable this river once had a channel through this bay into the ocean. The present mouth, however, is to

H. Ex. Doc. 114——3

the south of the bay, and it is blocked by a sand bar so as to effectually prevent ingress of vessels; but above the bar the Coquille river presents the character of a beautiful deep navigable canal, fit for steamers, for more than 50 miles of it course; and its valley, though narrow, has much good soil to recommend it. In the autumn of 1851 a force of our troops, under the immediate command of Lieutenant Colonel Casey, had a smart successful conflict with the Indians at the junction of the north and south forks of this river; one party of the command ascended in boats while the other proceeded by land; the pursued, in attempting to escape one, fell unexpectedly into the fire from the other, and were effectually chastised.

In regard to the Umpqua river, its mouth can be entered by sea steamers, under very favorable circumstances of wind and weather, also by small sail vessels; but it is not of a character to be regarded as a harbor, and it is only by light draft steamers that it can be safely ascended 24 miles or so up to near Scottsburg. Above this there is what is called the valley of the Umpqua, which is quite an extensive tract of most excellent soil. Should there be a good road opened from the head of navigation of this river into the valley it would add greatly to the value of this district of Oregon, and it would be useful for military purposes; and I think a good military road should be made between the mouth and Scottsburg.

Near the mouth of the Umpqua there was a Hudson Bay Company post, but now the site is occupied as a military post, established in the summer of 1856, by order of General Wool, when the detachment post at Port Orford was abandoned; the latter, however advantageous at the time when it was established, no longer being regarded necessary after the close of the Rogue River Indian hostilities and the removal of the tribes from their old homes to the coast reservations; but during the military operations which resulted in this removal the post at Port Orford proved of signal advantage, fully justifying the views of the officer under whose orders it was established.

From Crescent City to Rogue river, thence to Port Orford, the shore is broken and divided by spurs of the mountains coming quite down to the water's edge, throwing the mule track back from the sea up the steep sides and over the sharp crests of the spurs, making the route a very difficult one for the animals to tread; and yet it is the only land route connecting the shore settlements. Indeed, in almost all the country adjacent to the coast, and back into the interior as far as the Oregon trail, the roads generally are nothing more than pack trails for animals or foot paths for Indians and their pursuers.

With the exception of the valleys of the upper part of Rogue river, of the Umpqua, and of the Coquille, to which I have already made allusion, the whole country represented on map No. 9 is extremely forbidding to the eye of the farmer. Immediately on the coast the ground is covered with a dense forest of cedar, inferior pine, (called Oregon pine,) spruce, fir, &c., of trees of such gigantic size as to preclude the idea of clearing the land for cultivation. Further inland the back ground of this natural amphitheatral picture, viewed from the sea, is a succession of hills, then mountains of volcanic origin, rising one above the other, presenting their rocky fronts and sharp summits in beautiful shapes and variety of color, and showing their well defined crest line in clear relief against the sky as far as the eye can reach; and, as long as it can endure to observe, as we steam along the coast of Oregon, it will meet pretty nearly the same picture. The forest lands and mountain slopes of this coast will never be brought under cultivation. They are fit only for lumbering, and mining, perhaps, in some places. To the botanist, the florist, horticulturist, mineralogist, and geologist, they afford fields of interest, and, if explored, would probably yield many new and valuable specimens to their respective cabinets.

At Port Orford, which is just immediately south and under the cape bearing this name, there is a tolerable harbor, or rather, a "Hole in the shore," into which steamers of the largest class can safely enter and approach to within a few hundred feet of the beach, when the wind don't blow too hard from the south or southwest, and the fog is not too dense. Under a north or northwest wind, once in, vessels may ride at anchor here in security. This is not only the best, but it is the only place entitled to the name of harbor on the whole Oregon coast. A coast so strikingly destitute of harbors as this can contribute very little to the commercial prosperity of the State upon which it may front, presenting, as it were, a barrier rather than affording entrances to the interior.

Lumber is extensively manufactured by steam mills near Port Orford. It is here that the Oregon white cedar is found of an extraordinary size. Boards from three to five feet in width are produced of perfectly "clear stuff," and of such quality, for the plane, that this kind of lumber has, in a measure, superseded the white pine for interior finishing; for exterior work, however, it is not so well adapted.

On former official maps Cape Orford and Cape Blanco are put down as one; but Cape Blanco, whose approximate longitude 124° 45' W., and latitude about 42° 45' N., is distant from the former about ten miles. Between the two capes there is a beautiful indentation, bordered by a continuous sand beach, passable for wagons at all times, and affording the only wagon road passing out of Port Orford; all other routes leading out of this settlement can only be travelled on foot or on the backs of animals.

As soon as a military post was established at Port Orford attention was called to the advantage of having a direct communication with the Oregon trail. Several explorations were made with a view of finding a good route for a wagon road, but none were attended with favorable results for such a purpose. In the autumn of 1855 General Wool directed another effort to be made, and Lieutenant Kautz, 4th infantry, was put in charge of the party. The route which he reported most favorably upon as the least formidable in difficulties is represented on map No. 10.

While about closing his field labors his party was attacked by Indians—hostilities having commenced between them and the Oregon volunteers unbeknown to the lieutenant.

From my own reconnaissance in this district of southern Oregon, and other sources of information, I think the best system of roads that can be opened in order to bring the Rogue river, the Coquille, and the Umpqua valleys into communication with a sea-port would be—

1. To open a road on the direct route seen on map **No. 10**, from Port Orford to the Oregon trail.

2. To open one from Cape Blanco to the navigable part of the Coquille; also one from the head of the navigable part of this river, following the middle fork, to the Umpqua valley.

With such a system well executed these secluded valleys could avail themselves of Port Orford, as there is already by nature a good wagon road from this to Cape Blanco.

Cape Blanco, although possessing no harbor or "Hole in the shore," is not destitute of interest geographically, it being, I shall believe until more accurate observations prove the contrary, the most western point of terra firma belonging to the United States; certainly it is the most western habitable portion; not only is it habitable, but it is actually inhabited. squatted upon, and claimed by the "Bostons." From the fact of Captain Gray, the discoverer of the mouth of the Columbia, and his crew having sailed from Boston, this appellative was given them by the Indians, and extended to those since coming from the east to distinguish them from the Hudson Bay Company's people. Within the recollection of many now living the term "far west" was applied to no further than St. Louis, then the most westerly settlement of civilization. After that it became to mean somewhere about Independence, Mo.; thence climbing the eastern slope of the Rocky mountains and looking over its crest we saw it applied to the Mormon settlements of the Great Salt Lake basin. But here it rested only for a brief period; seemingly weary of resting place or local habitation, it departed from the city of polygamists, and with more wonderful strides than ever, crossing entire ranges of mountains, scaling with a bound the Sierra Nevada and the Cascade, traversing California and Oregon, it came to the Pacific. And here it is on the very brink of this ocean; and "far west" at this moment may be most legitimately applied to Cape Blanco. It is here that the Anglo-Saxon is arrested in his onward march by the broad Pacific. Westward the wheels of the emigrant wagon can roll no further. Another turn on their already well-worn axles and all are precipitated down the frightful steep of Cape Blanco a thousand feet into the deep bosom of the ocean. It is here that the cry of "Westward, ho!" by land must cease; and if on reaching this point the proneness for migration be not satiated, the journey further towards the setting sun must be on the ocean wave; or if migrate still our people will, thence by land must their course be in retrogression. Further than Cape Blanco I doubt if "Westward the march of empire hath its way," unless the "Bostons" can invent a bridge four thousand miles in span, and whose abutments shall be Cape Blanco and Cape Lopatka. Although there is still an onward migratory wave from the east to the west, a return wave has already begun to roll backward; and between the two—the direct and reflex—if we ourselves are not, another less fortunate race will be crushed—blotted out of existence—to make the way clear for the "Bostons."

Gold.—From the mouth of Rogue river to Cape Blanco, the point I have shown to be the "far west" of our country, the very sea-beach sand is full of gold dust; and in many places it has been washed, and a profitable return for the labor realized. In other spots it has been tried and abandoned, not from an absence of gold, but because of the smallness of the yield. At Rogue river and Cape Blanco large quantities have been obtained from the sand. The gold dust is an impalpable powder, so fine as not to be recognized with a microscope of ordinary power. To obtain it the sand is washed by a little stream of water, and while passing through a machine adapted to the purpose the dust is amalgamated with mercury, and afterwards placed in a crucible and the mercury of the amalgam driven off by heat, and the gold is realized in a solid form at the bottom of the crucible. Not only does this precious metal exist, in the form described, in the sea-beach sand, but it is found, in a more palpable form, however, in sand forty miles interior to the coast, (at Johnson's Diggins.) There is, however, a difference in the physical character of the two; that from the interior has crystals resembling the amethyst and also the topaz, which, though in small numbers and not perceptible to the naked eye, are brought into evidence by the microscope. Not so, however, in the beach sand; in this all the particles are black and the angles more rounded, owing to more attrition caused by the surf.

Gold is also found in Rogue River valley, on the Coquille branches, and undoubtedly exists pretty generally in spots all over the district under consideration; and it is this which has been the principal inducement for the whites to be willing to enter this district at so much hazard.

Indian hostilities.—This portion of southern Oregon has been the theatre of more Indian troubles than any other part of our Pacific possessions. The whole district represented on map No. 9 was full of Indians. Those more particularly occupying the valley of Rogue river have been regarded, since first known to the whites, as treacherous, brave, and energetic; and if at that time they did not know they were soon taught, by the whites themselves, how to use the rifle and revolver to good advantage. Notwithstanding all the evidences of danger staring them in the face, the whites underrated the skill, bravery, and local advantages possessed by the several tribes who occupied this district, as was the case in other parts of Oregon, and the first conflicts, as might have been expected, proved disastrous to the Bostons. One, probably the very first of these conflicts, I shall soon briefly describe; its result emboldened these Indians to defy, and inspired them with a reliance upon their own strength to effectually resist, the obtrusion of the whites into their country.

The scene of this rencounter was in the harbor of Port Orford. Between the mouth of Rogue river and Cape Orford there are scattered about in the bay many lofty rocks, towering high above the water in pyramidal form; isolated from each other by channels of deep sea water, they are the remaining solid portions, once of the land, that have been able to withstand the battering of the surf for ages. One of these is directly in the harbor, and possessed with historical interest. It is denominated Battle Rock, and stands so near in that at low tide it can be reached by wading; but it is only by one narrow face that it can be scaled, or its summit approached by the human foot. Once up, however, the top of the rock affords sufficient surface for a party of a score of men to stand on, or to ensconce themselves. It is probably 60 feet above the level of the sea. Usually upon a calm sunny day its summit is densely covered with a flock of sea birds, of all kinds, so different in color, shape, and size as to delight the ornithologist—some sitting, some standing, some apparently sleeping, some hopping, others flapping, screaming, crowding, and fighting, seemingly, to secure, each for himself, a momentary resting-place upon the rock; while high above all this din the atmosphere is darkened with myriads of the flock flying in all manner of gyrations—now ascending, next descending, some enlarging, others contracting the orbits of their flight—all looking down the while upon the angry strife of their fellows below, intently watching for the first vacant spot of the rock to suddenly dart down, seize, and perch upon it in turn, or contribute to the confusion. Such is but a feeble picture of the scenes with which the summits of these dark and towering pillars in Port Orford bay are daily animated. But upon the summit of Battle Rock a different strife from that of the birds was enacted.

In early times of the influx of population into California, immediately succeeding its acquisition to the United States, adventurous spirits to the number of a dozen or so chartered a schooner, and embarked at San Francisco, bent upon exploring the coast of Oregon, for purposes in general, and the purpose, in particular, of discovering a suitable site for a town, to be laid out into lots for sale. Arrived off what is now Port Orford, then not known to the Bostons, and attracted by the favorable aspect the site presented through the medium of their telescope, the schooner's prow was turned to the entrance of the bay, and when sufficiently in (about 10 o'clock, or five bells, a. m.) her anchor was let go, and she swung head to tide, then half ebb. The whole party, except the master and cabin-boy, were soon seated in the yawl, pulling ashore for a more minute examination. So engrossed were they in the discussion of speculative profits of "town lots for sale," little did they think there ever was such a thing as an ambuscade, or even dream of anything more, in the shape of an enemy, than a grizzly bear being near the handsome site that lay so invitingly before them. No sooner, however, had the party safely beached and secured their only boat above high-water mark, crossed the beach and fairly reached the high plateau, and began to admire the advantages of the site, when all of a sudden they were startled by a terrific yell in the rear, discovering the horrible reality of being completely surrounded and cut off from all access to the schooner by a hostile band of Indians, one party of whom being already in possession of their boat, and in all outnumbering the little band of adventurous speculators in "town lots for sale" ten to one. Here were symptoms unmistakeable of an enemy more formidable than grizzly bears; and if, perchance, there was a doubt of the intention of the Indians towards our little party it was but for a moment, as they were immediately saluted, in front and flank, by a shower of flint-headed arrows. This was promptly returned, but the Indians, nothing daunted, rushed furiously on, pouring in volleys of arrows as they advanced, and the fight soon became pressing. The little band of Bostons bravely and adroitly defended themselves, retreating until forced to the very water's edge, as it happened, directly under Battle Rock. The whites were not long in seeing that their last and only hope consisted in gaining its summit. In hasty council, amid showers of arrows poured in from their pursuers, it was decided to make the attempt to scale the rock. The effort proved successful, and, although possession was disputed by the countless number of sea birds which had held it undisturbed by any but their own kind for centuries, our friends, all eleven in number, thus separated from their schooner, some already wounded in the onslaught, found themselves on top of the citadel rock, and for a moment in comparative safety. The battle ceased, however, only long enough for the parties to survey their relative positions. The Indians, led on by their oldest chief, renowned in savage cunning, repeatedly attempted to scale the citadel, eager for the conflict hand to hand; but the Bostons defended the rock most successfully; every redskin venturing to scale it was a fatal mark for the unerring rifle or revolver. Their telling, well reserved fire and the flood tide at length gave the Bostons a respite, a breathing spell, for the first time since their surprise. It was not long, however, before they perceived their wily foe, the old chief, preparing to add to the attack a regular siege; and on looking for the schooner, with amazement beheld her fast sailing out of the bay. But before charging desertion, it must be told that the master, on discovering the ambuscade and becoming satisfied, although successful in baffling attempts of the Indians who had seized the yawl to board him, that he was powerless to render immediate aid by waiting, slipped his cable, and, by aid of his boy, hoisted sail and squared away before a fresh breeze for San Francisco, 375 miles before him, for assistance, that being the only point where it could be obtained. In this laudable undertaking we leave the schooner, and return to Battle Rock.

As soon as the next ebbing tide would permit the old chief returned to the assault of the citadel, but with no better success. In the meantime he had sent the swiftest runners to the remotest of the band, who, to the summons, came swarming in to swell the number of the besiegers. Every morning's dawn revealed to the unfortunate besieged a prospect more gloomy for each succeeding day. It was only during high water that it was not necessary to stand by their arms to prevent an escalade, which was as certain to be attempted as that low tide would ensue. The ravenous flock so unceremoniously dispossessed of their perch came circling and screaming around, excessively annoying them during the day, and the coming of night only afforded time for sad reflection in reference to the morrow.

For three days and as many nights, with several of their number wounded and bleeding, the heroic little band of "town lots for sale" speculators held the citadel, without food, without water, without rest, in the broiling sun of the day and in the cold damp of the night, against fearful and increasing odds. On the eve of the last night, their ammunition being very nearly exhausted, a council was held; it resulted in the bold, unanimous resolve, to make, under the cover of the dark, at low tide, the desperate effort to abandon the rock by the same narrow face they had gained it, and each for himself to run the gauntlet through the enemy's ranks, to seek, as a last resort, his own safety in the dark recesses of the woods immediately in rear of the Indians. At the proper stage of water that night this desperate attempt was made, and none, save one, ever escaped to tell the story of their disasters; he was two years subsequently found a poor maniac prisoner, in possession of the Coquille band. But what of the master of the schooner? He, true to his friends, returned with a strong party, after a trip of ten days, only, however, to find Battle Rock again in possession of its feathered occupants, and his friends beyond the reach of human succor.

The discovery of gold in the Rogue River valley attracted, with some well-disposed persons, many of the most unprincipled and ungovernable white men from all countries; with few exceptions, but for these wretches, it is believed the Indians of Oregon would have been the most peaceable, friendly, and easiest managed, with proper care, of any uncivilized tribes within the bounds of the United States. It is very true the Rogue river tribe was one of the few exceptions referred to; but they had felt the force of a blow administered by a command under Brevet Major P. Kearny, captain 1st dragoons in 1851, near the mouth of a branch of Rogue river about 15 miles north of Table Rock, (see map No. 11;) and whether this was sufficiently salutary or not, their roguish and stealing propensities afforded no just provocation, more especially when not in the commission of crime, for the infernal acts of cruelty committed upon them by some of that class of unprincipled whites, such as are always known to lurk on the confines of civilization, between the peaceable settlements and the Indian lodge, acknowledging no law but that of force, and in their hearts and acts far deeper down in the scale of human degradation, and far more capable of producing mischief in the settlements, because, to an evil heart, there is coupled superior intelligence, than any Rogue River Indian was known to be, before or since the discovery of gold in his valley.

Does any one ask what these infernal acts of cruelty have been? and by whom have they been perpetrated? Official public documents tell us: In the autumn of 1852, "a party of citizens, under conduct of one Captain Ben. Wright, massacred over thirty Indians out of forty-eight, who had come into his camp by invitation to make a ' peace.'"

It seems "Wright determined not to return to Yreka without bearing some evidence of success in his expedition, and having failed to find them by hunting for the Indians, he invited them to his camp by means of a squaw. Upon this invitation forty-eight came, and while there Wright directed his men to charge their rifles afresh, to make a sure fire, which was done in presence of the Indians, without exciting their suspicion, and then, upon a signal from Wright, they suddenly fired upon the Indians, and succeeded in killing about 38. The signal was the discharge of a revolver by Wright, by which he killed the two principal Indians, with whom he had been engaged in talk. Wright's men returned to town, bearing on their rifles the scalps of their victims, he reporting that he had demanded of the Indians stolen property, and on their refusal to deliver it up he had thus punished them."—(Ex. Doc. 76, 34th Cong., 3d session.)

As a natural result of this treachery, the tribe combined with the Rogue River Indians, in the following summer, and attacked a settlement near Jacksonville.—(See map No. 11.)

We thus have what are believed to be the provocation and beginning of the Rogue river war of 1853, terminating in a fight between the Oregon volunteers, with one captain and ten soldiers of the United States army, under General Jo. Lane, and the Indians, on the 24th September, 1853, on the side of the mountain seen on map No. 11, to the south of Battle creek.

Captain B. R. Alden, 4th United States infantry, had been ordered, in anticipation of any outbreak that might follow in consequence of the massacre by Wright, into that district; and promptly, on the first intimation, repaired with all the men, ten in number, of his company who were fit for duty, and before General Lane arrived, "the whole country had been scoured, under the direction of Captain Alden, in all directions, and the main body of the Indians driven to their strongholds in the mountains."

But this did not satisfy the volunteers; so, on the next day after General Lane joined the forces at Stewart's creek, he was elected to take command on the 22d of September. After assuming it he divided his force into two battalions, "in order to better scour the whole country," which he himself reports had already been scoured, and put one battalion under citizen Colonel Ross, and the other under Captain Alden, (who, be it observed, was an army officer, and had ten regulars,) and the general put himself at the head of this battalion, directing the one under Ross to proceed up Evans' creek, and Alden's to go *via* Table Rock, thence up the same creek.

The command started from Stewart's creek at 4 p. m., 22d September, and after pursuing the Indian trail under difficulties caused by the Indians setting fire to the woods in their rear, up Evans' creek, thence up Battle creek; the general reports that on the morning of the 24th, while riding in front, "he heard the crack of a rifle in the direction of the enemy," and without halting he advanced alone, and by his ear discovered their camp "in a dense forest thick with underbrush, which entirely obstructed the view."

When the troops came up the general announced his order of battle: "Alden, at the head of one company, to proceed on the trail to attack the enemy in front, and part of another company to go round and turn their left flank. Alden proceeded to engage them in the most gallant manner; his well directed fire was the first intimation of our approach. It being found impracticable to turn their left, the flanking party proceeded to engage them on their right. The men were now deployed, taking cover behind the trees, and the fight became general."

The general also reports: "I was delayed a few minutes for the arrival of the rear guard; these, all but fifteen, I immediately led into action. On arriving on the ground I found Captain Alden, who had been shot down early in the fight, dangerously wounded, in the arms of his faithful sergeant, surrounded by a few of his men. After examining the ground and finding that the enemy were securely posted behind trees and bogs and concealed by underbrush, and that it was possible to reach them, I determined to charge them. I passed the order, led forward in the movement, and within thirty yards of their position received a wound. Believing the shot came from the flank, I ordered our line to be extended to prevent the enemy from turning it, and the men were again ordered to cover behind trees." In this position, which they held for three or four hours, the general says that his "men were cool and determined on conquering." "Finding myself weak from the loss of blood, I retired to the rear to have my wound examined and dressed." While the general was in the rear the Indians cried to the whites "that they wished for a talk; that they desired to fight no longer; that they desired peace," and expressed a wish to see General Lane, who says: "Finding that they were much superior to us in numbers, having about 200 warriors well armed with rifles and muskets, well supplied with ammunition, and knowing that they could fight as long as they saw fit, and then safely retreat into a country exceedingly difficult of access, and being desirous of examining their position, I concluded to go among them."

During this interview the preliminaries of a peace were agreed upon. The treaty was completed at Table Rock a few days after; but it seems not until Captain A. J. Smith, 1st United States dragoons, arrived with his troop from Port Orford, were the negotiations for the peace concluded. General Lane says: "This arrival was most opportune."

It was soon after this that Fort Lane was established, and Captain Smith put in command. In speaking of the participators in this action, the general says: "Too much praise cannot be awarded to Captain Alden; the country is greatly indebted to him for the rapid organization of the forces when it was entirely without defence; his gallantry is sufficiently attested by his being dangerously wounded while charging at the head of his command almost at the enemy's lines." And then goes on to compliment, in the most flattering terms, the volunteers by whose voice he had been put in command; while it has been positively asserted that when the order to charge was given not a man of the volunteers advanced, but that Alden and his ten regulars charged unsustained. Ross' battalion did not arrive in time to participate in the fight, and only two companies, including the regulars, were engaged.

It will, I think, be perceived, on a careful examination of the general's report, that so far from a victory of the volunteers over the Indians having been gained, the latter were rather the victors; at the best it will not be regarded better for the whites than a drawn battle. The Indians asked for peace while yet in possession of the field, and obtained it. In granting it the general undoubtedly exercised sound judgment. He said, "I have no doubt, with a proper care, the peace can be strictly maintained;" and so it would have been, undoubtedly, but from causes similar in kind to that which provoked these hostilities.

The gallant general who figured as the hero of the closing scene of this three days' war was elected and took his seat in Congress as delegate from Oregon soon after, and during that Congress a large amount was appropriated to pay the volunteers who were in this service. The notorious Ben Wright not long after was appointed sub-Indian agent at Port Orford, and came to his death in the spring of 1855 by treachery at the hands of Indians on Rogue river—in their view a just retribution for his own treachery. Captain Alden soon after resigned his commission, and the army lost a gallant and meritorious officer.

Having presented the provocation, the progress, and conclusion of this affair, I leave it to others to infer what may have been the motives in superseding Captain Alden, and who were the gainers among the principal actors.

At the mouth of the Coquille river, "on the morning of the 28th of January, 1854, under the conduct of one Abbott, a recently discharged sergeant of the 1st dragoons, a party of whites attacked the different lodges of Indian families at daylight, before they were up, and sixteen Indians were killed and four wounded. The alleged cause was that the chief had threatened war; that he would not treat with the whites; that he had fired a shot at the house at the ferry, &c. The chief said he had fired at ducks' in the river, and not at the house." On investigation it was found that this was a wanton, unprovoked attack upon inoffensive families.

In July, 1855, a council was to be held by the then superintendent of Indian affairs in Oregon with the tribes in this district, at a point about three miles up from the mouth of Rogue river. The Indians, on invitation of the superintendent, were assembling. On the day previous to that fixed for the treaty one, from provocation, wounded a white man before the detachment of troops that had been sent from Port Orford to keep order had arrived. The whites assembled to the number of sixty, and loudly demanded of the sub-agent the offender, to hang him. This summary process was stoutly opposed by that functionary, but on the arrival of the troops he agreed to allow him to be taken under their conduct before a justice of the peace for a hearing. The justice bound the prisoner over for trial, and remanded him in charge of the corporal's guard to camp for safe custody. The corporal, with two privates, the prisoner, and another Indian as canoe-man, were returning in their canoe down the river, when they discovered a boat containing three whites in hot pursuit, and two others, containing whites, following. Soon the foremost came near the corporal's canoe and fired into his party, killing both Indians—the prisoner and canoe-man. Notwithstanding, the council was held, and the Indians of Rogue river and Port Orford agreed to quit their native soil and go to reside on a tract that had been designated as the Coast Indian Reservation, further north, represented on map No. 14. It was the design to gather all the bands along the coast of Oregon and place them upon it, there to teach them agriculture and the arts, and to forever prevent whites from acquiring the rights of soil upon it.

Now, it is certainly not to be denied that some of the Indians, especially in the upper part of the Rogue River valley, may have objected to the treaty, and evinced some reluctance to comply; but they had two years' time allowed in which they were to make preparations and go, and it is believed that had the whites shown patience and forborne to interfere the superintendent would have had them all removed within the time specified, and Oregon would have been saved the shame reflected upon her by the commission of those most outrageous deeds that followed; such, for example, as that perpetrated by one Lupton and his party, "who killed 25 friendly Indians, 18 of whom were women and children;" and that perpetrated by one Hank Brown and party, at Looking Glass prairie, "in killing from 8 to 10 friendly Indians, invited there by the settlers for protection and safety."

From such acts of cruelty can it be at all surprising that a retaliatory spirit was manifested on the part of the Indians?

We now have some of the provocations that in reality gave rise to the Rogue river war, of 1855, which was first formally and officially declared against the Indians, in the proclamation of George L. Curry, governor of Oregon Territory, October 15, 1855—assigning as the casus belli that he had been informed "that the Shasta and Rogue River Indians in southern Oregon, have, without respect to age or sex, murdered a large number of our people, burned their dwellings, and destroyed their property; and that they are now menacing the southern settlements with all the atrocities of savage warfare;" and by this same proclamation he calls out companies of mounted volunteers, to constitute two battalions—one to be denominated the "northern battalion," the other the "southern battalion."

The commanding officer at Fort Jones reported officially to the United States commanding general of the department, November 2, 1855, that "the recent murders by Indians of women and children in Rogue River valley, were literally retaliatory of, and immediately succeeded the massacre by Lupton and his party."

In confirmation of which we have the official letter of the adjutant general of Oregon, dated October 20, 1855, in which it says "information had been received that armed parties had taken the field in southern Oregon, with the avowed purpose of waging a war of extermination against the Indians in that section of the Territory, and had slaughtered, without respect to age or sex, a band of friendly Indians on their reservation, in despite of the authority of the Indian agent and the commanding officer of the United States troops stationed there."

Now, can any conscientious man believe that the intelligent, industrious officer, Captain Smith, who was then, and who had been, in command at Fort Lane, in the very centre of these Indians during the period of more than two years previous, would not have known, and reported to headquarters, a necessity, if there was one, of more military force than that of the United States already there to meet the exigency in the district of which he was the responsible commandant? No report was made by him or either of the commandants of Fort Jones or Fort Orford expressive of any such necessity.

The governor says he was moved to call out this force "by a petition numerously signed by citizens of Umpqua valley," and ordered them to rendezvous at Jacksonville, which is the identical focus of the organization of General Joseph Lane's volunteers of 1853, who had been so liberally paid by the United States from an appropriation disbursed among them just previously to the getting up of this moving petition, which, if granted, would bring occupation for eight hundred men and as many horses for the ensuing winter, and they would only have to ride about and kill Indians until planting time next spring. These battalions, with the title of "southern army," were under the command of Brigadier General John K. Lamerick, and it is not surprising that with such an array and the well known hostility of many of the citizens, some of the Indians flew to their arms and others to the United States military posts for protection.

On rendering his report of March 31, 1853, General Lamerick only cites three skirmishes, in which he claims success for the several divisions of his army; of these, one was with Old John's band of about 200, while on the trail to Crescent City, in which the enemy retreated fighting to the mountains; 3 whites and 10 Indians killed; another, when 100 volunteers attacked 75 to 80, on Cow creek, and drove them; one white killed and one wounded; four Indians killed; the third was when a company attacked 75 Indians, six miles south of Camos prairie, and drove them, killing three. But he makes no allusion to the shameful conduct of the 250 volunteers who had agreed to support Captain Smith's regulars in the fight of Grave Creek hills, where, by a single blow, had these volunteers come up to the work, the war would probably have been brought to a close in 15 days after the issuing of the governor's proclamation; nor does he report other affairs of more shame to the "southern army" during the succeeding winter, of which some are enumerated in an official report by the commanding general of the department of the Pacific, May 30, 1856.

He says "no man can have felt more keenly or grieved more sincerely than I have at the sacrifice in southern Oregon of many innocent men, women, and children by savage warfare. But what was the cause? No other than the massacre by volunteers and citizen of soms 80 or more friendly Indians. As in the case of the killing, by two companies of volunteers, a friendly chief (Old Jake) and his band, comprising between 30 and 40 males, besides destroying their huts and provisions, and exposing their women and children to the cold of December, who, in making their way to Fort Lane for protection, arrived there with their limbs frozen; the killing in the most brutal manner, with clubs, two old squaws, one of whom was lame and carrying a child, which was taken by the heels and its brains dashed out against a tree; that of the same Brown who was concerned in the massacre by Lupton, during which an Indian boy, twelve years of age, who could speak some English, ran to him and said 'I have done you no harm, my heart is good towards you, you will not kill me.' Brown replied 'Damn your Indian heart,' and seized him by the hair and with his bowie knife severed his head from his body; the determination of certain citizens to murder 400 friendly Indians at Fort Lane, waiting there to be conducted by the superintendent of Indian affairs to the coast reservation, but prevented by Captain Smith, the commanding officer; the similar determination in the Willamette valley to kill the same Indians, and all who might accompany them, should the attempt be make to take them to the reservation.''

It has already been said that an immediate effect of the organization of the governor's southern army was to cause some of the Indians to stand to their arms, one of their first acts afterwards was to attack the little party of 10 under Lieut. Kautz, 4th infantry, when about closing the exploration for a road from Port Orford to the Oregon trail in the direction of Fort Lane, (see maps Nos. 10, 12.)

In this attack, which occurred on the 25th October, 1855, at a point marked with that date on the map, the lieutenant made a successful defence without serious hurt, and the party made their way safely to Fort Lane, this officer having, in the mean time, discovered the position of the main body of Indians then under arms to be in the Grave Creek hills, about 45 miles from Fort Lane.

All the disposable troops at the fort were put in motion. The command of regulars consisted of 85 men and 4 officers: Capt. A. J. Smith, 1st dragoons; First Lieutenant H. G. Gibson, 3d artillery; Second Lieutenants A. V. Kautz, 4th infantry, and B. Alston, 1st dragoons. At Grave creek they were joined by 250 volunteers, under Colonel Ross. From this point they moved in three detachments by different routes towards the position of the Indians. Unfortunately, from an error of the scouts in regard to the location, all three detachments came up in front instead of on different sides of the Indian camp. About daylight 31st October the regulars, accompanied by two companies of the volunteers, after climbing very steep and difficult hills, came in sight of the Indians. Fires were then imprudently built, which gave the Indians warning. At this point the baggage and provisions were left in charge of Lieutenant Alston. The command descending a mountain gorge, and climbing the opposite acclivity, came upon the Indians, charged and drove them from the crest of the hill on which they were encamped and some 50 yards into the brush over the crest.

From the top of the hill for a distance of $1\frac{1}{2}$ mile it was a dense thicket; on the left and on the right there was a precipitous descent into a gorge filled with large pines, with undergrowth, in which the Indians concealed themselves, and all efforts to dislodge them proved futile. Several charges were made by the regulars, but the men were picked off so effectually by the Indian rifles that but little advance was made into the thicket. The regulars stood their ground well, but the volunteers, with the exception of about fifty, were of no benefit in the action.

The troops continued to occupy this position until near sunset, now and then exchanging shots with the Indians. After posting pickets the troops descended to a spring to bivouac for the night, their loss during the day having been thirty killed and wounded. The next morning Lieutenant Gibson, with ten men, was sent up the hill to bring down the dead body of one of his detachment; this had barely been accomplished when the Indians came in large force around, and after exchanging numerous shots, with but little effect, save the wounding of Lieutenant Gibson, for two or three hours, were driven off, and left the troops in possession of the field. At noon on the 1st November Captain Smith having found by his experience the day before that no confidence could be placed in the promised support of the volunteers, ordered a return to Fort Lane, which was reached the next day.

The number of Indians was estimated at 300. The number of troops actually engaged did not exceed 120, with every disadvantage of position. The Indian loss, according to their own admission afterwards, was 7 killed. The greater portion of the regulars were dragoons, and their musketoons proved utterly inadequate to cope with the rifles in the hands of the Indians.

No effort of Captain Smith could persuade the volunteers to go round and take the Indians in the rear, while the regulars would charge in front, and it seems only 50 out of 250 of the volunteers of the governor's southern army could be induced to take any part in the action, after coming to the point where, with resolution, they could have been instrumental in capturing the whole body of Indians in arms.

In the case of this southern army of Oregon we have the example of a governor of a Territory organizing a military force, with a general officer at its head, and sending it into a field within the command assigned by the President to a general officer of the United States army; the said governor in the mean while not so much as condescending to inform the President's officer of the measure, nor of the orders, it now appears, he issued to the volunteers which prescribed the relations they were to hold with the United States troops regularly stationed in the same field. It was only by accident, as it were, in the following month the United States officer commanding the department of the Pacific obtained a knowledge of the governor's military measures. To say nothing of the question of the legality of those measures, one familiar with military usage cannot fail to perceive in them either a marked contempt of the authority of the President's commander of the department, or else a total want of knowledge of that courtesy which of right and by usage is due to such officer.

On the 9th of the same November, while Major General Wool, United States army, in command of the department of the Pacific, was at Crescent City, on his way to the field of Indian hostilities, which had broken out in the preceding month in the Yakama country to the north of the Columbia, he received the first intelligence of the fight just described, and it was then that he also first received authentic information of the governor's declaration of war, and of the southern army of his volunteers being in existence.

General Wool's presence in southern Oregon at this juncture was exceedingly opportune.   He was personally in position to enable himself to judge of the necessary measures to be taken for the future duties that would properly devolve on the troops under his own command in this district.   Accordingly, acting upon the basis of humanity towards the Indians, and at the same time having a due regard to the safety of the settlements, the commanding officers of the United States army in this district were instructed during the winter to receive at their posts and protect from violence all friendly Indians who would come in and express a willingness to go in the following spring on the reservation set apart for them.

In spite, or more probably in consequence, of the operations of the governor's southern army during the winter, it turned out in the spring that the number of Indians in arms had increased; that they had the entire command of the lower part of Rogue river; were besieging a block-house filled with citizens near the mouth, and were really threatening the destruction of all the whites there; while many of the friendly Indians had repaired to Crescent City, Fort Orford, and Fort Lane for the promised protection, and to be ready to move according to the terms of the treaty.

Several bands, deemed unfriendly, were in arms at different places in the valley above; among these was that of Old John, who said "the whites are determined to kill me and my band and we may as well die fighting as in any other way."   Indeed, this band alone had become so formidable as to defy the "southern army;" and finally it became necessary for the superintendent of Indian affairs, and for the safety of the settlers, to call upon the regular troops to end the troubles on Rogue river.

Accordingly, General Wool, being previously well advised of the topography of the district, and the probable positions of the bands in arms, devised and put into execution the following plan of military operations for ending this Rogue river war by the United States troops.   After sending a detachment of troops from Fort Lane to guard and conduct the friendly Indians waiting there to the reservation, there was left a small disposable force under Captain Smith, 1st dragoons.

One company (Captain Augur's, 4th infantry) was ordered down from the Columbia river to Port Orford, where Captain (Brevet Major) Reynold's company, 3d artillery, was already stationed; as soon as Augur's could arrive there would be troops enough to protect the friendly Indians and public stores collected here, and leave another small force disposable for the field.

Captain Floyd Jones' company, 4th infantry, was ordered from Fort Humboldt to Crescent City, to protect all supplies and public property that might be landed there, also to guard the friendly Indians who had been gathered there by the superintendent of Indian affairs in Oregon.

Captain Ord's company, 3d artillery, then stationed at Benicia, was ordered to be in condition for field service, and in readiness to embark at a certain time in the steamer from San Francisco to Oregon.

Brevet Lieutenant Colonel Buchanan, junior, major 4th infantry, was selected by the general as the commanding officer to execute the plan of field operations.

On the 5th of March the general himself embarked with Ord's company, Lieutenant Colonel Buchanan, and a few officers of his staff; Captain Cram, Corps Topgraphical Engineers; Lieutenants Bonny-castle and Arnold, aids-de-camp, and Assistant Surgeon Milhau, for the field of operations; and while on his way up explained very fully to Lieutenant Colonel Buchanan the plan he desired him to execute. Lieutenant Bonnycastle subsequently relinquished his appointment as aid, and joined the force in the field.

Ord's company was to land at Crescent City, and the movement to commence from there as soon as it would be judged that the force from Fort Lane under Captain Smith, he having been advised, should be able to reach the Illinois river, see map No. 9; and the force at Port Orford was to proceed towards Rogue river, all three being subject to the orders of Lieutenant Colonel Buchanan.

The general believed that by starting the three forces, all tending ultimately to meet somewhere near the mouth of the Illinois river, that from Crescent City moving towards the mouth of Rogue river, that from Port Orford towards the same, or to a point higher up, and after uniting both to ascend the river, while Captain Smith's would be descending the valley, all the hostile bands would be most likely to be encountered or ferreted out. He was aware of the natural difficulties of the ground, and of the severe labor the troops must apply to the task.

The field of operations is represented on map No. 12, and the points where engagements occurred are designated by the symbol of two swords crossed.

On the 8th of March Lieutenant Colonel Buchanan landed at Crescent City, and in one week after had his command in motion. The force from Crescent City left on the 15th and encamped at the mouth of Rogue river (Ord's company skirmishing there with the Indians) on the 20th of March.

And now it was that most of these Indians began to show signs of yielding, but their chiefs were tardy in coming in. The McAnooteney band were obstinate; their town was 11 miles above the mouth, on the right bank, (seen on the map,) at the entrance of a small stream from the west. On the 26th of April Ord's and Jones' companies, 112 men, Captain Ord, Captain Jones, Lieutenant Drisdale, and Doctor Millman, were sent up to raze that town; it was destroyed, but not without obstinate resistance. The Indians were in force, and, having the advantage of descent and cover, attacked the troops in flank and rear. It was a spirited fight, resulting in the Indians being driven up and across the river; then the troops withdrew in good order, losing Sergeant Nash, however, who was shot from the bush, and ar-rived in camp the next night.

H. Ex. Doc. 114——4

On the 29th of April Captain Ord's company moved from camp at an early hour and encountered the Indians on the Chetco river, where he found them in force on the right bank. A running fight ensued; the Indians, running faster than the pursuers, succeeded in crossing the river and dispersing themselves in the hills.

Captain Smith's force had descended the valley from Fort Lane, and the chief in command had consented to hold a council, he, as well as the superintendent of Indian affairs, hoping that all now standing aloof might be induced, after the lessons already received, to come in, lay down their arms, and go upon the reserve.

Oak Flat, on the right bank of the Illinois, was designated as the council ground, and there the council was held on the 21st and 22d of May, the result of which was that most of the Indians agreed to come in, and three days were allowed them to rendezvous at Big Meadow, above the Big Bend of Rogue river, where they were to deliver up their arms, and thence to be escorted by the troops to Port Orford. All but Old John's band promised to come in with seeming sincerity.

The whole command, except Ord's company, were present at the council; that had previously been sent to Port Orford to escort a provision train to Oak Flat, and as it had not arrived, Reynolds' company was despatched, by the trail seen to the south of Pilot Knob, to meet it should it come by this route; but it came by the mouth of the river, thence on the east side. It was highly important to protect this train, without risking an attack.

On the 24th Captain Smith, with 50 dragoons and 30 of the 4th infantry, 80 in all, left the council ground for Big Meadows, to receive the arms and to escort the Indians to Port Orford; it was probably intended to conduct them thither by the most direct trail, after opening or improving it, from the Meadows. Smith had crossed the river and encamped at the point marked C on the evening of the 26th, Augur's company having accompanied him nearly there to escort a train back. On the day of Augur's return, probably the 25th, the chief in command moved from Oak Flat down the Illinois, leaving Jones' company at its mouth, and himself, with Augur's company, crossed Rogue River and went up to a point marked B, about three to five miles west, to open or improve the direct trail, to which I have referred, from Big Meadows.

It will now be seen that on the evening of the 26th of May Lieutenant Colonel Buchanan's forces were situated: himself, with Augur, at the point B; Ord, escorting the train, on the east side of Rogue river, within about ten miles of Oak Flat; Jones, at the junction of the Illinois; Reynolds, about ten miles from that junction, on the Port Orford trail; Smith, at Big Meadows, at the point C; and the main body of the Indians were about five miles above the meadows, on the bank of the river.

It had rained very hard all day the 26th, and this was assigned to Captain Smith as the reason why the Indians had not arrived at the place of rendezvous. As the rain had rendered the trails muddy, this seemed a reasonable excuse, and he trusted they would all be in by the close of the following day.

Battle at Big Meadows.

As before stated, Captain Smith was encamped, on the evening of the 25th of May, at the point C; but before many hours had elapsed, that same night, circumstances occurred causing him to distrust the Indians, and he immediately commenced moving his camp, and by midnight his command were occupying a much better position—an oblong elevation, 250 yards in length by 20 in width, represented on map No. 13, between two small creeks entering the river from the northwest. This is a mound of low elevation, and between it and the river there is a narrow bottom, which is Big Meadows. The southern border of the mound is abrupt and very difficult to climb; the northern border more difficult; the west end is approachable, and can be ascended with some difficulty, while the eastern is a gentle slope, easy of ascent. The top is a plateau of an area sufficient for one company to encamp on. Directly to the north there is another mound, about the same size, covered with scattering trees and brush. The summits of the two are within rifle range, and at about the same elevation.

Early on the morning of the 27th Smith despatched an express to apprise Lieutenant Colonel Buchanan of his new position, and that the Indians had not come in, and said to the express, "I think Old John may attack me." It is to be observed that this chief had not assented to the agreement of the others. The express reached his destination that afternoon. The lieutenant colonel sent him back to Smith, and requested to be informed if he desired to be reinforced. The express, however, could not reach Captain Smith, and, finding he was surrounded by Indians fighting furiously, returned, but, getting lost during the night, did not report to Lieutenant Colonel Buchanan until 10 o'clock the next morning, (28th of May.)

The chief in command immediately called in Augur's company, (then cutting a road,) and ordered it to join Captain Smith at the Big Meadows. The shortness of the time in which Captain Augur executed this order proved that gallant officer to be equal to the emergency. The distance, on the very difficult foot trail, is nearly eighteen miles, and it was accomplished in four and a half hours. In the mean time stirring scenes were being enacted at the Big Meadow mounds.

Smith's command had been up all night moving his camp, and, notwithstanding his men were much fatigued in consequence, by dawn of day his position was defensible. After starting the express off, and as the morning light increased, numerous parties of Indians were seen coming from all directions, and soon the north mound was occupied by a large number.

A body of 40 warriors came up the gentle slope of the east end of the mound, occupied by the troops, as if to enter camp. They signified a wish to see Captain Smith, as they said, to give up their arms to him; but that officer was on his guard, and directed them to deposit their arms outside, designating a spot where all the Indians must lay down their weapons. It afterwards appeared that this was a stratagem to seize the person of Captain Smith. By the precaution already taken of planting a field howitzer so as to sweep that slope, and of stationing Lieutenant Switzer with the infantry, to defend at all hazards the crest of the western slope, he was in condition to make good his refusal to allow the warriors to enter his camp, and after a short colloquy they retired, and were seen to hold consultation with their chiefs on the opposite mound, where it had been discovered Old John was very active in giving orders.

It was now apparent to Captain Smith that an attack was meditated soon to be made upon his position. At 10 o'clock on the morning of the 27th May, the Indians having completely surrounded, opened a smart fire upon it, and simultaneously charges were made up each slope, upon his flanks, but these were repulsed with the howitzer and infantry. Now the voice of Old John rose above all others, issuing his commands in tones so clear that they were distinctly heard in Smith's camp, and interpreted to him. During the day this master spirit frequently ordered a chage to be made by his warriors, and it was attempted, but as successfully repulsed as the first. The Indians were continually firing rifle shots from all quarters into Smith's camp, and parties often boldly attempted to scale the steeps of his mound, which protected his front and rear. In these desperate efforts at escalade, which gave the troops ample work to resist, several Indians on coming near enough were made to fall, roll over and bite the dust. Only 30 of Smith's men had arms at all adapted to long range: the 50 dragoon musketoons could only tell when the enemy came near. The Indians were much better armed and delivered effective shots, themselves unharmed, comparatively, from the north mound. The battle was thus prolonged till night.

During the night of the 27th Smith rendered the position of his men more safe from the enemy's rifles, by digging pits and erecting breast defences, such as they were, with his few articles of camp equipage.

On the morning of the 28th the Indians, refreshed, and augumented in numbers, again opened fire upon the troops, and the battle was continued pretty much in the same manner as it had been the day previous. Old John could be heard above all the din shouting, urging, encouraging, and even cursing his warriors to stimulate them to a renewal of the desperate charges, which, as often as attempted, were successfully repulsed, while Smith's men were now less annoyed by the rifle shots of their enemies. The troops were directed by their officers to husband well their ammunition, and never to make a shot unless there was a fair prospect of its telling. But the shots from the north mound had told sadly upon the little command, and Assistant Surgeon Crane had his hands full. The dead and the wounded numbering 29.

About 4 o'clock p. m. the Indians were observed to be forming, under the direction of "Old John," in two bodies, apparently with a view to charge both flanks simultaneously, as well as the front and rear, at the same time with an unsual number. Smith was not mistaken in this conjecture; soon they were seen advancing, and the flanking parties were half way up, Smith, in the mean time, while giving orders to his men how to act in this emergency, caught glimpses in the distance of approaching numbers. Augur's company had come ! and that officer gallantly entered the arena leading his men at double quick, charging the Indians in rear. At the same moment Smith, for the first time, ordered a charge from his right and from his left down both slopes of his mound, upon the advancing foes. And now it was that the commanding voice of their chief was heard no more, the Indians broke and endeavored to escape by crossing the river, and victory declared for the troops.

The number of warriors who had arranged themselves under the banner of Old John for this last struggle for the defence of their valley was about 400.

This chief was known to be brave and capable to command. He had planned his operations well and extensively. After learning of the scattered positions of the forces under Lieutenant Colonel Buchanan, he counted upon destroying Smith's command on the morning of the 27th in a short time; then to immediately descend and attack Jones, at the mouth of the Illinois, before Augur's company, being on the opposite side of Rogue river, at some distance, and Reynolds, at a still greater distance, could come to the rescue; and then to cross the Illinois river and attack Ord and capture his train. So confident were his warriors that Smith would fall an easy prey that they had pieces of rope to the number of Smith's men in readiness to hang every one.

On the 29th, the next day after their defeat, the Indians sent word to Captain Smith that they wanted "a talk." On the 30th the lieutenant colonel in command arrived at Big Meadows with his whole force. The Indians again agreed to come in and go upon the reserve. Old John was the last to give in, but finally assented.

About 20 miles above the mouth of Rogue river Captain Augur had another fight with a party, about the 8th June, and brought them in; and by the last of June the Rogue river war was at an end, and all the Indians that had defied the "southern army" of Oregon so successfully were either at or on their way to the coast reservation in western Oregon.

The expectations General Wool had entertained of the officer who was selected for the command in this important service were fully realized, and the manner in which his plan for closing this war was executed by Brevet Lieutenant Colonel Buchanan met the general's entire approbation.

Western Oregon.—Map No. 14 shows so much of this as includes the coast Indian reservation, and the military posts Umpqua, Hoskins, and Yamhill, and the upper part of the Willamette. These three posts were established by General Wool's orders in July, 1856, for the purpose of guarding the Indians, in number about 1,500, whom his humane measures had been instrumental in moving to this reservation. After the removal of these Indians from the Rogue river valley and Port Orford district, it was no longer necessary to maintain troops at Fort Lane or Fort Orford. The positions occupied by the new posts, considering the mountain passes through which the

Indians could escape and return to their old grounds, were believed to be the best that could have been selected to prevent their escape and at the same time to afford protection to the settlements in this part of the Willamette and to the Umpqua valleys. The reservation is about 72 miles in length, coastwise, and 24 miles in average width, extending from the Pacific back to the summit ridge of the Coast range of mountains.

Should it be deemed expedient Fort Hoskins might be moved into the reserve and placed on the Siletz, at a prairie seen marked on the map at P.

From November to June steamers ascend the Willamette to Corvalis, and to Dayton on the Yamhill during the whole year. The roads are passable for wagons between Fort Hoskins and the neighboring towns.

Distances.

From—	To—	Miles.
Fort Hoskins	Corvalis	15
Do	Salem	30
Do	Dalles	20
Do	Fort Yamhill, Grand Rond	40
Do	Dayton	40
Do	Portland	68
Do	Fort Vancouver	75

The Willamette is tributary to and enters the Columbia about 6 miles below Fort Vancouver. Its general course is north, parallel to the seacoast. Sea steamers of 10 feet draught ascend to the city of Portland, 12 miles above its mouth, and 144 miles by the steamers' run above the bar of the Columbia. Above Portland the Willamette becomes of less depth, so that small river boats are used to ascend 12 miles to Oregon City; at this point navigation is interrupted by the "Willamette falls." Here the whole river comes tumbling in majestic grandeur over the rocky barrier, making the total fall 30 feet vertical in a short distance. Above these falls, for a distance of 50 to 55 miles to Salem, the stream is navigated by light draught steamers in favorable stages, and even to Corvalis between November and June.

The valley of the Willamette is about 120 miles in length, north and south, and about 36 miles in breadth, east and west, giving about 4,100 square miles, most of which is good for agricultural purposes. This valley is the trough between the parallel mountain ranges, the Cascade on the east and the Coast range on the west side, and it is one of the very best in Oregon, whether we consider its magnitude, climate, soil, or facilities of outlet. Wheat, barley, oats, potatoes, apples, and pears are raised in great abundance, and it would sustain a population of 150,000. Its products might be immense in proportion to its area; but where would a market be found for its surplus?

Distances by the roads.

From—	To—	Miles.
Fort Lane, (Rogue river valley)	Booneville	181
Booneville	Corvalis	5
Corvalis	Albany	10
Albany	Santiam	8
Santiam	Salem	15
Salem	Oregon City	36
Oregon City	Portland	11
Portland	Fort Vancouver ferry, Columbia	8

The military connexions by road between northern California, and southern and western Oregon, are as follows going north in—

Distances.

From—	To—	Miles.
Fort Jones, *via* Yreka, California	Fort Lane, Rogue River valley, Oregon	69
Fort Lane	Evans' ferry, across Rogue riv...do	11
Jacksonville	Evans' ferry ...do	23
Evans' ferry	Grave creek ...do	19
Grave creek	Cow creek, Umpqua valley...do	9
Cow creek	Eliff, south extremity cañon ...do	7
Eliff	Cañonville, north ext'y cañon...do	11
Cañonville	Myrtle creek ...do	10
Myrtle creek	Round Prairie ...do	8
Round Prairie	Roseburg, (Deer creek)...do	7
Roseburg	Winchester ...do	5
Winchester	Catapooy creek ...do	9
Catapooy creek	You Calla...do	11
You Calla	Mouth Pass creek ...do	7
Fort Umpqua	Scottsburg ...do	24
Scottsburg	Elkton ...do	20
Elkton	Mouth Pass creek ...do	15
Mouth Pass creek	Eugene City, Willamette valley...do	30
You Calla	Siuslaw, (Long Tom creek) ...do	30
Siuslaw	Starr's Point ...do	30
Starr's Point	Jennyapolis ...do	8
Jennyapolis	Booneville ...do	3
Booneville	Fort Vancouver, (ferry, Columbia)	93
Fort Jones	Fort Lane	69
Fort Lane	Fort Hoskins	201
Fort Lane	Fort Vancouver, (ferry)	274
Fort Yamhill, Grand Rond	Fort Vancouver, (ferry)	55
Fort Umpqua	Fort Hoskins	146

There is a wagon road from Fort Jones to Fort Lane, crossing the Ciskiou mountain, which is bad to pass before the 1st to the 10th June. When it is in good condition it takes three days for a wagon to pass between the two forts.

From Fort Lane a company of dragoons marched to Fort Vancouver ferry on the Columbia river, by the route above given, in 21 days in the month of November, when the roads were very heavy, taking its wagon train along. This was at the rate of 13 miles per day.

From Fort Umpqua, *via* Scottsburg and the Long Tom creek, to Fort Hoskins the road in many places on the first part of the route would be very difficult to march a command over. I have already referred to the importance of improving this part by an expenditure from the public treasury for military purposes. I have no doubt if a good road were opened on this route one of the three posts now required to guard the coast reservation might be dispensed with.

Northern Oregon.—The part of this as far to the eastward as Fort Dalles is shown on map No. 16; thence to where the parallel of 46 degrees of north latitude strikes the Columbia is shown on map No. 20. The length of the portion of the Columbia which is in part the northern boundary of Oregon is about 345 miles; that is, from its mouth up to the point where it is met by that parallel 5 miles below the old Hudson Bay post, Fort Walla-Walla. This same portion also makes a part of the southern boundary of Washington Territory. From the said point, about 5 miles below Fort Walla-Walla, in going eastward, the boundary between the two Territories is that parallel of latitude continued to the summit of the Rocky mountains.

The Columbia is successfully navigated by a sea steamer, entering its mouth under the charge of a pilot in fair weather at high tide, drawing 18 feet water, up to Fort Vancouver, a United States military post on its right bank, 138 miles above the bar; and by one of 10 feet draft up to the Cascades, which are 45 miles further up the river. At the Cascades all navigation is effectually stopped by rapids and falls, in which, for an extent of $4\frac{1}{2}$ miles, the total fall is $27\frac{1}{2}$ feet. In the pool of the river, extending 45 miles from the head of these falls to Fort Dalles, on the left bank, the river is again navigable by small river steamers. From Fort Dalles up to the head Des Chutes for 15 miles navigation is stopped by rapids; thence the river is again navigated by oar boats about 100 miles, to Fort Walla-Walla, and this reach is not interrupted by rapids for 60 miles further up.

From the mouth to Fort Dalles, 233 miles, the valley of the Columbia seems to partake more of the character of a crack or cleft in the earth produced by volcanic violence than by any other cause. There is very little of the soil that is at all desirable for cultivation. There is plenty of timber of poor quality, fir, and Oregon pine and miserable oak on the islands, but not a tree grows there that is fit for ship building, except for small spars or yards. The lumber that is made from these forests is of a coarse kind, answering for only the frame work of buildings.

To one who has personally examined the physical character on the ground, rather than judged by the physical geography as presented by the few maps, which are only distinguished by their paucity of information of the vast region drained by the Columbia, the idea is irresistible that it can never become one in which civilization can flourish. This is the general view to be taken of Oregon from the Pacific to the summit of the Rocky mountain range. It is true there are valleys and spots, and even some hill-sides which, but for the formidable physical barriers separating them, would be desirable. Such obstacles as the Sierra Nevada, the Cascade range, and the Coast range of mountains running across a State, render all intercommunication almost impossible without vast expense, and their sterile sides and broad bases leave but a small fraction of the total soil fit for cultivation. The number of square miles in Oregon is nearly 172,000. Of this area there is not more than 40,000 square miles at all fit for cultivation, even supposing good markets for surplus and easy intercommunication. But from the eternal barriers separating the little fertile valleys, the difficulties of access, the want of harbors and markets, not more than one-eighth part of the whole soil of Oregon can be regarded as at all adapted to agricultural industry of any profit. These isolated valleys are exceptions to the general rule of barrenness or sterility which attaches to the vast region drained by the Columbia—a region only fit, as a general rule, for the occupancy of the nomadic tribes who now roam over it, and who should be allowed peacefully to remain in its possession.

The Columbia river is important for military purposes in connexion with these tribes. On this line we are now keeping up a post at Vancouver, Cascades, Dalles, and Mill creek; the last, however, being some 30 miles to the south of the Columbia, in the valley of the Walla-Walla.

Only one of these, Fort Dalles, is in Oregon; but it is an important point. It is to the Pacific slope what Fort Leavenworth is to the east slope of the Rocky mountains in its military aspect. In all the country above the Dalles mounted troops may be used to advantage; but to give the employment of such more economy a communication should be made from Fort Vancouver along the banks of the Columbia of a nature to allow a troop of dragoons to pass along it by their own feet, without the necessity, as now, of transporting the animals in boats. On this subject I here quote what I have said on a former occasion: "Congress appropriated for a military road from Fort Vancouver to Fort Dalles. I am satisfied, from my own reconnaissance, a good wagon road on the banks of the Columbia between these two points cannot be well and properly made short of $450,000. And even supposing it made at this cost, the principal part of the transportation for military purposes would continue to be done by steamboats. But there is an improvement that could be made in the bad places on the existing trail, consisting in improving this trail into a road that will enable dragoons to pass readily over it at all seasons. It would then save the great cost now incurred for the transportation of horses, mules, and cattle upon steamers for military purposes. The sum of $25,000 would be ample for this kind of improvement; and it is precisely what is wanted by emigrants and stock growers to drive their stock on down the Columbia."

I have already said there are no steamboats now navigating any part of the Columbia above Fort Dalles, and above it, in any direction into the Indian country, transportation must be by land for all military purposes, except in that direction which would be accommodated by row boatsabove Des Chutes.

The district of northern Oregon, lying between the bases of the Cascade range and the Blue mountains, has much sameness all the way from Fort Dalles to the Umatilla, (map No. 20.) It is high and rolling prairie and bears good grass. It cannot be said to be well watered, although water occurs at convenient distances along the road. The streams are approached by steep descents, and are generally fringed with cottonwood. In all other places the country is destitute of timber. In the immediate valleys of the streams the soil is often fertile, but these valleys in no case exceed half a mile in width. The tributaries of the Umatilla become almost dry in the fall, and that river itself becomes a mere rivulet in September. Along the base of the Blue mountains are numerous springs, which always yield a supply.

The whole region of country embracing the valley of the Umatilla, and those of its tributaries, is well adapted to grazing.

The road between Fort Dalles and the west base of the Blue mountains is as good as natural roads generally are in hilly prairie districts. This is the road followed in passing between Fort Dalles and the military post in the Walla-Walla valley. A judicious expenditure of $25,000 on this road would make it good for all purposes. The distance between the two posts is 164 miles to go round by McKay's, on the Umatilla. From Fort Dalles to the Indian agency on the Umatilla it is 111 miles; and from Fort Dalles to the spring at west base of Blue mountains it is 143 miles.

Distance from—	To—	Miles.
Fort Dalles	Des Chutes river	15
Des Chutes river	John Day's river	28
John Day's river	Cedar spring	6
Cedar spring	Willow creek	18
Willow creek	Butter creek	33
Butter creek	Umatilla Indian agency	8
Umatilla Indian agency	Spring on Umatilla	5
Spring on Umatilla	McKay's, on Umatilla	15
McKay's	Spring west base Blue mountain	15

Eastern Oregon is shown, on map No. 15, so far as to include an extensive district of country lying between the Blue mountains and the Rocky mountains, presenting the lower part of the Snake river, and the headwaters of the Salmon river. This map exhibits the topographical features of a considerable extent of Indian country hitherto little known, except at a few points along the emigrant road.

In the summer of 1854 a party of emigrants, on their way towards the Pacific, were attacked and several massacred by Indians in the Fort Boisé district. In May, 1855, Major General Wool, commanding the department of the Pacific, repaired to Fort Vancouver, on the Columbia, and organized an expedition consisting of an equivalent of two mounted companies, with instructions to proceed into the Fort Boisé district, with a view to protecting the immigrants that might be on their way; also to apprehend and bring to justice the Indians who committed that massacre. Lieutenant Mendell, Corps Topographical Engineers, then serving in my party, was designated as the topographical engineer officer to accompany the command for the purpose of making a reconnaissance of the country. This map (No. 15,) gives the topography obtained during all the movements of the command. All the objects contemplated by the general in organizing and sending out this expedition, under Brevet Major G. O. Fuller, captain fourth infantry, were fully realized through the energy of the officers and men composing the command. Not only were the offending Indians apprehended, tried, convicted, and executed, but protection was afforded to immigrants and much valuable information of the tribes and country they occupy was obtained. The moral effect produced upon the Indians in this region of country was decidedly beneficial in restraining their subsequent conduct

From the west base of the Blue mountains to Powder river.—In going eastward, after leaving the Umatilla, we begin immediately the crossing of the Blue mountains, which divide the waters flowing into the Snake from those running into the Columbia. The road is hard upon both animals and wagons. After attaining to a height of 1,500 feet we come upon undulating table lands, heavily timbered, with occasional prairies of good grass. From the snow and rain falling upon these mountains the Columbia derives no insignificant share of her waters conveyed to her by many streams heading in them. Locked within these mountains is the valley called Grand Rond, of irregular shape, from seven to twelve miles wide. Its soil is good, bearing excellent grass, and it is well watered by a river bearing its own name. It is the best valley in the whole country shown on this map; it is the favorite summer resort of several tribes of Indians whose, winter homes are on the west side of the Blue mountains. It was in this valley that, in the summer of 1856, the "strike," to use his own word, was made by Lieutenant Colonel Shaw of the Washington volunteers. He reports that "with 160 men and officers he charged the Indians assembled there on the morning of the 17th July, near their village, and dispersed them, following and killing them, until they hid themselves in the rocky cañons." From his own report of his killed and wounded, however, it may be a question whether his party obtained a victory, especially considering his previous threat : "If I find them I will strike them, and follow them until I drive them out of the country;" the fact that he reports "it impossible to state how many of the enemy were killed;" and the remaining fact that he did not follow them into their hiding places, although his men were mounted and armed.

This exploit may be regarded as the last "strike" of the Washington volunteer army raised by the governor of that Territory, and sent June 8 to the Walla-Walla valley. Unfortunately for the glory of this achievement, it has been reported that "the whole object was to plunder the Indians of their horses and cattle, and provoke a prolongation of the war." On learning the destiny of Lieutenant Colonel Shaw's force the general officer of the United States army commanding the department instructed Colonel Wright, 9th infantry, to "order all the volunteers out of the country by the way of the Dalles, and if they do not go immediately they will be arrested, disarmed, and sent out."

Distance from—	To—	Miles.
Spring, west base Blue mountains	Lee's encampment	14
Lee's encampment	Grand Rond river	17
Grand Rond river	West end Grand Rond valley	6
West end Grand Rond valley	South end valley	7
South end valley	Divide Rond and Powder rivers	4
Divide of Rond and Powder rivers	Powder river crossing	13
West base Blue mountains	Powder river	61

It is apparent that the Grand Rond valley affords an excellent position for a number of troops to remain in, should occasion require it, for some time.

From Powder river to Kamas Prairie.—The artemisia, or sage bush, is found in profusion over the whole of this district, giving a most desolate aspect to the landscape in which it prevails. It grows in light, sandy soil, that produces nothing else.

On Burnt river the hills are high and grassy, leaving narrow valleys between. The road is very hilly and circuitous, crossing the stream nine times before leaving it, at very rocky places; the road follows down the stream to near its mouth, and then strikes Snake river, which is the south branch of the Columbia, and drains all the country lying to the south and east of the Blue mountains even to the Rocky mountains.

Fort Boisé, on the right bank of the Snake, is but a small adobe house, with a few articles of traffic. It is regarded as an important station. There are several small islands here in the river, which are fertile and well timbered.

Boisé river enters the Snake just above the fort. It is large, and not fordable here at high water. The emigrant road is along this river. Fifty miles above the mouth the road leaves the river to avoid a deep cañon; still further to the eastward, where the road again comes to the river, it is again seen running through a similar chasm of basaltic rock 300 to 500 feet deep.

Seventy miles from Fort Boisé a road called "Jeffrie's Cut-off" departs from the old emigrant road, and runs *via* Kamas Prairie to Fort Hall, an Indian trading post. It is a new route, and compares unfavorably with the old, except in grass, in which it is superior. Between the old road and Kamas Prairie, it is very rugged and broken.

Kamas Prairie is a long narrow plain, of irregular width, from 15 miles at its western to a narrow neck at its eastern extremity, and about 68 miles long, from east to west. It is bounded on the north by a high range, separating its waters from those running into the Boisé, and on the south by another ridge of less height. The plain has some timber at its eastern end; it is watered by numerous streams uniting and discharging themselves into the Malade river, which passes by its eastern extremity. Most of the small streams of this prairie become nearly dry in summer: "One, upon which the command encamped in the afternoon, was found perfectly dry next morning; shortly, however, it commenced to run again with undiminished vigor." The mountains to the north of the prairie are well timbered, but in the plain there is only birch and willow. Kamas is found here in great abundance, which is so much used as food by the Indians; it grows spontaneously in low, moist, light soil. This prairie is a great resort for Indians, there being good grazing and plenty of animals; such as foxes, rabbits, and grouse.

From our military post on Mill creek, in the valley of the Walla-Walla, established by direction of General Wool, in 1856, *via* McKay's, to the spring at the west base of the Blue mountains, it is about fifty miles, and the road is good for wagons. This post is the nearest military position we have occupied to the Indian country in eastern Oregon. The distance between it and the west end of the Grand Rond is about 80 miles. A command of mounted men could perform the march in four days with its appropriate train.

From the same post to Fort Boisé it is about 224 miles. This could be marched by a command of two or three companies in twenty days with its appropriate wagon train. Good camping grounds with excellent grass and good water would be met at convenient distances for the daily marches all the way any time between 1st June and 15th November.

Distance from—	To—	Miles.
Crossing of Powder river	South slough Powder river	12
South slough Powder river	Fork of Burnt river	14
Fork of Burnt river	Last crossing Burnt river	39
Last crossing Burnt river	Snake river	4
Snake river	Birch creek	3
Birch creek	Sulphur spring	10
Sulphur spring	Malheur river	13
Malheur river	Fort Boisé	18
Fort Boisé	West extremity Jeffries' Cut-off	70
West extremity Jeffries' Cut-off	West extremity Kamas Prairie	30
West extremity Kamas Prairie	East extremity Kamas Prairie	65
Powder river	Fort Boisé	113
Fort Boisé	West extremity Kamas Prairie	110
Fort Dalles	Fort Boisé	317
Fort Dalles	West extremity Kamas Prairie	417
East extremity Kamas Prairie	Godin's river, (*via* Jeffries' route)	60
Godin's river	Fort Hall	43
Fort Hall	Great Salt Lake City	183
Fort Dalles	Fort Hall	583
Fort Dalles	Great Salt Lake City	768

From Kamas Prairie to Salmon Falls, on Snake river, 40 miles, the route is by a trail impracticable for wagons. Along the south base of the south ridge bounding the prairie is a remarkable belt of huge basaltic rocks, of more than one mile in width and of length unknown. The rocks are of grotesque shapes, standing at distances from 20 to 30 feet apart, and in height from 10 to 40 feet. They are worn smooth, as if by the action of water. The trail winds through the belt. From this to Snake river it is a pavement of basalt cut up by deep ravines, or a stretch of artemisia.

A few miles before reaching the Snake we come to the Malade river, flowing between vertical walls of basalt, no fringe of timber marking its presence.

There are two falls on the Snake called Salmon Falls; they are five miles apart; the lower has a descent of 25 to 30, and the upper of 10 to 12 feet. Here the Indians catch large quantities of salmon and dry them for winter use.

From Kamas Prairie to Lemhi, on Mormon river, 125 miles, the route is impracticable for wagons. The larger portion of the country is mountainous, the trail often very rocky, and none but well shod animals should attempt it. Good camping spots, water and grass are plenty. From the eastern extremity of the prairie the route is up the Malade river, at the headwaters of which it crosses a mountain range thickly timbered with fir, at a considerable depression, which is 2,500 feet above the valley, and then strikes the headwaters of Godin's river. The valleys of both of these streams are narrow but grow wider as we descend them. Godin's runs in a northeasterly direction over a pebbly bed until deflected by mountains at right angles to its former course, and then runs towards the largest of the "Three Buttes," near which it sinks.

A high divide pierced by two low gaps separates Godin's river from the Pash-a-mu-rah river. At the north base of this divide there is "a stream of ice-cold water rising vertically from the ground and flowing in different directions and uniting below, forming an island a mile in length and several hundred yards in width. The eye can distinguish no dividing ridge between the streams, each of which was 4 feet wide and 6 inches deep. As they flow further they are increased probably by fresh accessions rising from the ground."

Pash-a-mu-rah is a tributary of Salmon river, and waters the valley called McKay's Hole, signifying a valley surrounded by mountains. This is 8 to 10 miles broad and 30 miles long, bearing excellent grass at its northern extremity, and there it has a fishery.

The next considerable valley is that of the most easterly of the large tributaries of Salmon river. In this the Mormons, at a distance of 320 miles from Great Salt Lake City, have established their settlement Lemhi, on Mormon river, 20 miles above its junction with the Salmon, and 136 miles northward of Fort Hall.

Mormon River valley, though several thousand feet above the level of the sea, is fertile, and the settlement promises to be of some importance. The grazing is excellent and winter mild. Limestone and coal are said to exist. The mountains are timbered, and cottonwood grows in the valley. A wagon road, nearly level, connects it with Salt Lake City, *via* Fort Hall. Lemhi is a missionary station among the Indians, and is furnished with a stockaded enclosure. The settlers, to all appearance, are orderly and certainly very industrious, and devoted to their peculiar principles of religion.

The situation they have selected is eminently favorable. Numerous Indians winter in this valley, while many more pass through in transitu for the buffalo grounds east of the Rocky mountains.

This valley would be a good location for a military post, should future exigencies demand one in this part of Oregon. The Mormons think a wagon route is practicable from Lemhi to the Flathead Indian country, where it is also their intention to establish a mission.

Nature has furnished this region more abundantly with game than is her custom along the eastern tributaries of the Columbia; such as bears, including the grizzly, deer, antelope, elk, and mountain sheep; the latter is much in favor as food for the Indians. One band of the Shoshonees is called Tu-chu-re-kay, meaning sheep-eaters. Various kinds of grouse are among the smaller game. It is not long since buffalo fed in the valleys of this region, but the improvident Indians have either exterminated them or driven the herds to the ranges east of the Rocky mountains.

From the mouth of the Mormon up to the head of Salmon river, 100 miles; thence to the Pash-e-wah-kite, 58 miles: thence via Payette river, 87 miles, to Fort Boisé.

The trail on this route is only practicable for pack trains. Good camping places and good water and grass occur at convenient distances for daily marches.

At the junction of the Pash-a-mu-rah the Salmon river has a wide valley bearing luxuriant grass. On ascending, however, the valley is found more contracted and the trail more hilly. The river heads in a lake, one mile or so in circumference, on the top of a very high ridge, upon which there was snow in August.

The country on the Salmon is the best of any on the route followed by the command, except the Grand Rond. "But it is only a good country by comparison. In a region where most of the earth's surface is either rugged mountains or desert plains a strip of alluvial soil, be it ever so narrow, is apt to be over-appreciated."

From the head lake of the Salmon a dividing ridge is to be crossed to reach the Moo-rum-ba, which heads in several small lakes. It is but a short distance across the ridge. The mountains here are covered with dense forests of fir extending down the plain.

The Moo-rum-ba was followed down to where it emerges through the mountains to the north. Thence the route was up one of its tributaries; leaving which it crossed several others of its tributaries and entered the valley of the Pash-e-wah-kite. The west branch of this is about fifty-eight miles from the head lake of the Salmon. In this reach the route is necessarily tedious and circuitous, in consequence of numerous high rugged mountains, obliging the traveller to follow the water-courses.　In these valleys the nights were cold, producing ice in August.

The Pash-e-wah-kite is one of the prettiest of all these valleys. It is a plain some fifteen miles long, in some places with excellent soil, in others it is pebbly and sandy.　It is watered by a bold stream 15 to 20 yards wide, of delightful cool water.　Pines and firs are scattered through it, giving an abundance of shade.　The mountains on all sides are high and covered with dense forests.　It was in this valley that Lieutenant Day's subdivision of the command killed several of the participants of the Fort Boisé massacre.　This was an important event, teaching the survivors that our troops could penetrate their most remote recesses and inflict deserved punishment.

From the west branch of the Pash-e-wah-kite to Payette river it is twenty-eight miles; thence following down this stream to the fishery it is twenty-four miles; thence the route continued still down the valley fifteen miles to a point some twenty miles above its mouth; from that point it is an artemisia plain for twenty miles directly across to Fort Boisé.

Indians in eastern Oregon.—Lieutenant Mendell thinks it a matter of congratulation for ourselves that the districts of country just described are not inhabited by a bold race of Indians disposed to war on the whites.　The high rugged mountains of their country would afford a thousand refuges to them, while interposing great obstacles to pursuers.　Nature provides them with food, which they have only to stretch forth their hands to receive, even to the very sources of the streams.　Free from hunger, with such a country extending very far in every direction, with every foot of which they are familiar, it would be exceedingly difficult to carry on hostilities with them from our remote settlements with success.　They resort to the buffalo country in summer and return in the fall.　They are much inferior in energy and intelligence to those west of the Blue mountains.　They are believed to have once been a powerful nation, occupying the waters of the Missouri, but a long and bloody strife with the Sioux drove them to the west of the Rocky mountains, and here they have deteriorated. They still cherish their enmity to their old enemies, the Sioux, and live in great fear of the Blackfeet tribe.　They steal many horses from the Cayuses, who occupy the west base of the Blue mountains, and from Nez Percés, and are in turn robbed by the Blackfeet.　They are of filthy habits, eating beetles and vermin with gusto, and are very poor, often suffering hunger in winter from their improvidence. On such occasions they live upon their horses, and a case is known of one who in a season of want killed his squaw and five children, and jerked them for his winter provision.

MILITARY CONNEXION BETWEEN NORTHEASTERN OREGON AND UTAH.

From the interesting journal kept by Major O. Cross, of the Quartermaster's Department, of the march of the rifle regiment from Fort Leavenworth, *via* South Pass and Fort Hall, to Fort Dalles, on the Columbia, in 1849, I am enabled to present some practical information in reference to a march of a command, if required from northern Oregon to Great Salt Lake City.

From Fort Dalles to south extremity of Grand Rond Prairie the march would be 187 miles, which could be accomplished in 14 days; from Grand Rond to Fort Boisé, 130 miles, in 10 days; from Fort Boisé to Fort Hall, 268 miles, in 22 days; from Fort Hall to Great Salt Lake City, 183 miles, in 15 days.

A regiment leaving Fort Dalles with its train could reach Salt Lake City in 61 days. The proper time for starting would be from the 1st to 15th June.

A regiment could be despatched from New Orleans by steamer, *via* Panama, and conveyed to San Francisco in 23 days; thence to Fort Dalles in 7 days; thence, if the train were held in readiness there to start immediately, the same regiment could start the following day, and march to Salt Lake City in 61 days, after arriving at Fort Dalles, making 91 days from New Orleans, by the way of the Atlantic, the Pacific, and Columbia river, to Great Salt Lake City. Lieutenant Colonel Steptoe's command was 92 days marching from Fort Leavenworth to Salt Lake City in 1854.

VII.—*Military considerations in reference to the Washington Territory portion of the department of the Pacific.*

Map No. 16 shows all that portion of the Territory lying west of the Cascade Mountain range.

Leaving the mouth of the Columbia, and proceeding along the coast northward, we pass Shoal Water bay and Gray's harbor, and arrive at Cape Flattery without perceiving anything at all that would invite one to become a settler on this part of the coast. From Cape Hancock, at the mouth of the Columbia, to Cape Flattery, by the steamer's shortest run, it is 149 miles. From San Francisco the latter cape is 793 miles. Just around on the inside of the cape there is an Indian village, in which the houses are built of stone. These Indians have the character of being pretty honest and peaceable.

Passing up the Straits of Fuca we leave Vancouver's Island on our left; at the head of these straits, turning south, we come to Port Townsend, where we have a military post, about 110 miles from Cape Flattery. Opposite this post is Whidbey's island, one of the most important of our own in all these waters.

Leaving Port Townsend, and going still further south, we pass through Admiralty inlet and come to Fort Steilacoom, a military post on Puget's Sound, 215 miles by the steamer's run from Cape Flattery. From Fort Steilacoom, 30 miles by the road, to the northeast, is the military post at Muckle Chute prairie, on White river. From Fort Steilacoom, by the road, it is 25 miles in a southeast direction to Olympia, the capital of the Territory, situated at the southernmost extremity of the Puget's Sound waters.

H. Ex. Doc. 114——5

After running up the Straits of Fuca for about 90 miles, if we turn north and pass through the Straits of Haro, we enter the Gulf of Georgia; thence turning east we come to Bellingham Bay, where is also a military post, which, by this route, is about 160 miles from Cape Flattery.

From Port Townsend direct, by water, to the post at Bellingham Bay, through the Rosario straits, it is from 60 to 70 miles; and from Fort Steilacoom, through these straits, to the Bellingham Bay post, it is about 150 miles. These posts can easily communicate with each other by water, as also with San Francisco; but the communication with each other by land is very difficult, owing to dense woods, the want of roads, and the very circuitous routes that have to be followed in consequence of the numerous little bays and watercourses.

The waters in this part of Washington may be assimilated to inland seas in some respects, and in others to broad navigable rivers. They open by the Straits of Fuca and Gulf of Georgia into the North Pacific, and have directly in their front the British island, (Vancouver,) of which Victoria is the principal town and harbor. The numerous channels, bays, straits, and inlets, form an extent of navigable waters of several hundreds of miles either for sail or steam vessels and Indian canoes of great size. There are many excellent harbors. In these waters canoes are used capable of carrying from 20 to 80 warriors, with their arms, and they are adapted either for catching the whale or for war, and are of such speed that a sail vessel is of no use in the pursuit. In case of difficulties with these Indians, a steamer of the capacity to carry two companies of troops, and of a speed of 10 to 15 miles per hour, would be of more service than a whole regiment without such means of rapid transit.

The shores of these waters are very generally covered with heavy timber—fir, cedar, and pine of inferior quality for everything except spars, yards, piles, and the frames of buildings. In all Washington Territory it is yet to be ascertained whether there is a tree growing fit for ship-building purposes, other than for those named, or fit for the lumber required for floors and the finishing of buildings.

The clearing of the timber lands for farms is not to be thought of; and those who expect to find extensive prairie tracts in this part of the Territory, for agriculture on a large scale, will be egregiously disappointed. I do not mean to say there are no spots, for there are some that will produce well in this part of the hitherto much overrated terrestrial strip called Washington Territory, extending from the 113th to the 125th degree of longitude, and from the 46th to the 49th degree of latitude, in all containing 130,000 square miles of the earth's surface. Of this whole area not more than one-eighth part is at all adapted to general agriculture. Similar causes to those explained for Oregon prevent intercommunication between the parts separated by mountain ranges as we go eastward to the summit ridge of the Rocky mountains, which is its eastern boundary.

In the acquisition of this strip of territory, it is certainly not to be denied, by any sensible man who has examined it carefully, that the United States realized from Great Britain but very little that is at all valuable or useful to civilized man. For the Indians, but for the presence of the whites, it would ever have remained well adapted.

In Bellingham Bay coal mining is successfully carried on to some extent; the coal is light in weight, burns freely, and the quality of the article is altogether similar to that at Coos bay, in Oregon, described in the preceding chapter. This business at Bellingham Bay, the lumbering and fishing business in other parts of the Washington coast, are about all that occupy the people, except so many as are engaged in the cultivation of soil sufficient to produce what may be needed for home consumption, and except those engaged as government officials. The whole number of white male inhabitants in the Territory does not exceed 1,700. The lands on the river bottoms, west of the Cascade range, are so densely timbered that, no matter how rich, they will not be brought under cultivation for many generations to come, if ever. Cereal grains, except Indian corn, grow well in many places, and the wheat is excellent in quality.

From Fort Steilacoom, 25 miles by the road, in a southeasterly direction, the capital of the Territory, Olympia, is situated at the southernmost extremity of the Puget's Sound waters. There are two ways of reaching this from San Francisco—one by sea, 1,038 miles, through the Straits of Fuca, Admiralty inlet, and Puget's Sound; the other is by sea to the mouth of the Columbia; thence up this river 65 miles to Rainier; thence by the Cowlitz river 28 miles to its head of navigation; thence by land 60 miles; the total distance by this last, which is the mail route from San Francisco to Olympia, is 775 miles. The part of this route from Rainier is the main channel of communication between the Columbia river and Olympia. The distance from Fort Vancouver by this way to Fort Steilacoom is 186 miles; and it is a very difficult one for troops to pass over at any season, more especially at all times other than midsummer.

It is very evident that in a Territory a scattered population, not exceeding that of a respectable sized village, cannot be expected to defend themselves in their peaceful occupations against so large a body of Indians as are known to exist in Washigton, without the presence of United States troops in considerable numbers. The question then arises as to the most effectual way of rendering adequate defence?

For the purpose of the most perfect and economical defence for the portion west of the Cascade range, I am of the opinion that a permanent post should bo established on Puget's Sound, near old Fort Nisqually, of sufficient accommodations for two companies. There is an excellent harbor here, at which a good dock could be built; and from the dock to the post a good road should be constructed, the length of which would not exceed one mile. At Port Townsend there should be stationed two companies, and a post of two companies maintained at Bellingham Bay.

These troops, with the use of such a steamer as suggested, would hold in check not only the warlike Indians, who come down in their great war canoes from the British possessions, but they would preserve peace between those within our own limits and the whites.

"In the end it will prove a great extravagance in the government to neglect the proper defence of a remote frontier like this; and one chief reason is, that, if so neglected, a pretext will always be afforded to a territorial executive to incur an extravagant and unnecessary expenditure" by calling out the volunteers.

After the Indian troubles had been closed by the United States troops in this district, in the summer of 1856, the commanding general of the department directed the posting of one company at Port Townsend, and one at Bellingham Bay, these being all the troops that could then be spared to place there.

Passes of the Cascade Range of Mountains.—There are four of these, viz: the Klikatat, the Cowlitz, the Nachess, and the Yakama, (or Snoqualme,) having Indian trails by which communication is held between the tribes occupying the districts on both sides of this range. These passes are impassable in winter on account of snow, and not until about the 10th of June are they practicable for troops. The Nachess and Yakama are the most important. They connect the Puget's Sound with the Yakama district.—(See map No. 17.) A military road was improved so that wagons could pass from Fort Steilacoom through the Nachess, *via* Selah fishery, to Fort Walla-Walla. But it has been so much neglected and damaged by floods that it is now impracticable for wagons in many places.

For military purposes it is highly desirable that a road should be kept in condition across the Cascade range for communicating between the Yakama valley and Puget's Sound. The best pass for this purpose is the Yakama, and not the Nachess. The road should follow the valley of the Yakama river, down through the Kittetas, to the Selah fishery. It could probably be opened through the pass, and other difficult places improved sufficiently to allow a wagon to pass, for the sum of $125,000, with the aid of a body of troops for escort service.

A road opened as suggested, and the post at Muckle Chute prairie advanced up to the base of the mountains near the Yakama Pass, and one established in the Kittetas valley, we should be in a position to hold the Indians in submission throughout all the Yakama country, as well as those all along the west base of the Cascade range.

Fort Simco, seen a little to the north of the Topinish, the proposed post in the Kittetas valley, and Fort Dalles, would be in easy communication. From Fort Simco, 50 miles to the point where the Yakama river is cut by the 47th parallel of north latitude, in the Kittetas valley, a good wagon road would cost $50,000, and from Fort Dalles, 60 miles to Fort Simco, such a road would cost $15,000.

The Selah fishery and the Kittetas district may be regarded as the heart of the Yakama Indian country, in which there are excellent grazing, good fishing, and an abundance of water. This fishery is the principal one on the river, and the Kittetas is a good valley, 20 to 25 miles in diameter, and well watered by several branches of the Yakama: and I doubt if there will ever be any necessity for a military post further north than the point referred to in this region of our possessions; it would be within 1° in latitude of the British possessions.

The whole Yakama country should be left in the quiet possession of the Yakama and Klikatat Indians. Colonel Wright, 9th infantry, who, while in command of this district, carefully examined the question, on the ground, among these very Indians, says: "They require all this country: they cannot live at any one point the whole year. The roots, the berries, and the fish, make up their principal subsistence; these are all obtained at different places and in different seasons of the year. Hence they are frequently changing their abodes until fall, when they descend from the mountain districts, and establish themselves in the lower valleys for the winter."

In reference only to the tribes occupying the valleys of the Yakama and Klikatat, Fort Simco is sufficiently advanced in a direction north of Fort Dalles, (map No. 18.) But, in reference to the great Indian thoroughfare from Selah fishery, through the Yakama Pass, and the communication that ought to be kept up with the Puget's Sound district, the post recommended to be established in the Kittetas will be important. The only objection to the site indicated may be a deficiency of building timber immediately on the spot; but excellent yellow pine is found in abundance on the Yakama just above, which can be floated down.

From the spot which would probably be selected for the post, through the pass to a position proper for the post on the west side, it would probably not exceed 70 miles. The distance by the valley from the point of the river where it is cut by the 47th parallel to Lake Kitchelas, near the summit of the Yakama Pass, is about 60 miles, and the valley is well wooded with pine, fir, and cedar; below that point, for 50 miles down, cottonwood and willow; thence for 40 miles to the mouth of the Yakama there is no wood.

Distance from—	To—	Miles.
Fort Steilacoom	Puyallup river	23
Puyallup river	White river, (Porter's prairie)	9
White river, Porter's prairie	Post at Muckle Chute prairie	3
White river, (1st crossing)	Green river, (1st crossing)	30
Green river, (1st crossing)	Green river, (last crossing, base mountains)	12
West base mountains	Last prairie on summit	6
Prairie, summit Nachess Pass	First crossing Nachess river	2
Fort Steilacoom, through Nachess Pass	First crossing Nachess river	85
First crossing Nachess river	Last crossing Nachess river	27
Last crossing Nachess river	Winass river	10
Winass river	Leaving of Winass river	16
Leaving Winass	Selah fishery, Yakama river	4
Fort Dalles	Topinish, (Haller's field)	58
Fort Dalles	Fort Simco	60
Fort Simco	A-tah-nan Mission	12
A-tah-nan Mission	Selah fishery	30
Fort Steilacoom	Selah fishery	142
Selah fishery	Hudson Bay Co.'s post, Walla-Walla	95

With regard to the posts now on the Columbia river, at Vancouver, and the Cascades, (map No. 19,) it is to be remarked that, as a military point in reference to the command of the river, in respect to Indian difficulties, the latter is of more importance than the former. This is a great Indian fishery, and there should be no hindrance offered to prevent these people from resorting here for this purpose, at the same time order should be preserved. It is a point where all supplies by water have to be transhipped and carted over a portage five miles in length; there should be two companies stationed here. Fort Vancouver is well adapted for depot purposes, and one company stationed there for a guard will be amply sufficient.

Portland, on the Willamette, will continue to be, as it is now, the commercial centre in this district, unless it shall prove, on a proper survey of the Columbia, that sea steamers can at all times ascend to the foot of the Cascades.

The general commanding the department directed a military topographical reconnaissance to be made of the valleys of the Walla-Walla and Touchet. The report was such that the practiced eye of this officer at once perceived that not only for the then existing war, but likewise for future operations and disposition of troops, one of these valleys should be occupied as a military post. Accordingly one was established in the first named, five miles below Whitman's old mill site, (map 20,) on Mill creek.

The importance of this post cannot be questioned by one familiar with the topography and localities of the many tribes in advance of this position, and of the disposition of the encroaching whites, ever prone and ever ready to thrust themselves into the Indian country in advance of the proper frontier line. The War Department may rest assured this post will have to be maintained for years to come, and the sooner a good wagon road be made between it and Fort Dalles, the more money, in the end, will be saved to the quartermaster's department

I here quote from an able report of the late Secretary of War what I regard as especially applicable to the Walla-Walla valley: "Instead of dispersing the troops to form small garrisons at numerous posts, where they exhibit only weakness to the savage foe, it is suggested that, within the fertile regions, a few points accessible by steamboats or by railways should be selected, at which large garrisons should be maintained, and from which strong detachments should annually be sent out into the Indian country during the season when the grass will suffice to support cavalry horses and beasts of draught and burden."

At present there is little need of a post further advanced from Fort Dalles into the Indian country than the one now on Mill creek, in that direction, provided this be properly garrisoned.

General Wool reported, October 23, 1854, a post beyond the Walla-Walla valley "would subject the government to a very heavy expense to keep it properly supplied. I would prefer a company of dragoons to traverse the country in the neighborhood of Fort Boisé during the summer, and at the approach of winter return to Fort Dalles and remain till spring. To supply the company with effective

(American) horses, such as the service requires, would cost in this country a very large sum of money."

The post in question is on the trails leading into the Pelouse, Nez Percé, Spokane, Snake, and other Indian countries, and it should be occupied with six companies at least. This would allow of two detachments (two companies in each) to be sent out every season from here into the vast Indian country lying east of the meridian of this post, on the various routes explained under the heads "Eastern Oregon," chapter VI, and Eastern Washington, chapter VII. A garrison to the number suggested once posted here, it would not be long before a river steamer would be plying between the Des Chutes and the mouth of Walla-Walla. In connexion, I offer one more suggestion, which is, that the breed of Indian horses now in the Walla-Walla country, being inured to grass alone, shall be fairly tried by the mounted troops in those annual expeditions. With proper treatment these horses may be foraged all winter without grain, and do good service in summer upon their native grass.

Distance from—	To—	Miles.
Fort Dalles	Indian agency on Umatilla	111
Fort Dalles	McKay's, on Umatilla	129
McKay's, on Umatilla	Military post, Mill creek	40
Military post, Mill creek	Mouth Walla-Walla river	20
Fort Dalles	Military post on Mill creek	169

To make the road good from Fort Dalles, *via* McKay's, to Mill creek post, for wagons, $15,000 would be required. A more direct route could be opened between the two posts, but it would cost more and would not subserve so many purposes as the one named.

It will be perceived that the foregoing suggestions for keeping peace in all Washington Territory and all along on the north border of Oregon involve—

1. The maintaining of a two company post at Port Townsend, and a like one at Bellingham Bay; the moving of the Steilacoom post to the Nisqually, and here establishing a two company post and depot, the moving of the Muckle Chute post to near the west extremity of the Yakama (Snoqualme) Pass, to a point commanding the pass, the valley of Cedar river, and the trail from the pass down the Snoqualme river. In this position of the post there should be two companies to garrison it. The town of Seattle would be the nearest seaport, and 60 to 70 miles distant.

2. The keeping of a suitable government steamer in the Washington waters capable of carrying two companies, and running (faster than the northern war canoes) at least 10 miles per hour.

3. The maintaining of Fort Vancouver as a depot with one company, and a two company post at the Cascades; the establishment of a new post in the Kittetas valley, with two companies; the maintaining of Fort Simco, with two companies; also Fort Dalles, with two companies; and Mill creek post, with six companies.

4. Appropriations of money: $125,000 to open a road through Yakama Pass from Snoqualme falls, or from a point on Cedar river to the Kittetas, on the Yakama river; $50,000 for one from Fort Simco to the Kittetas; $15,000 for improving the military road between Fort Dalles and Fort Simco; $25,000 for rendering the trail from the Cascades, on the bank of the Columbia, passable for dragoons to Fort Dalles; $15,000 for improving the military road between Fort Dalles and the Mill creek post; in all, $230,000 for military roads, all in Washington Territory, except a part of the last one named.

It will be seen I do not propose to increase, except by one, the number of posts now occupied; there are nine now, and the plan proposes ten; one additional and a change in the localities of two, furnishing each with a proper number of troops, 23 companies in all, and opening proper roads to enable communication to be kept up between them.

With the 23 companies located as proposed, and such communications, peace may undoubtedly be maintained for a long time to come throughout Washington Territory, the eastern and northern portions of Oregon, for the whole extent of the Snake and Columbia rivers.

With a less number of companies, I am willing to admit, Indian hostilities might be suppressed after breaking out, as has been proved by the result of General Wool's plans for terminating so successfully those of 1855–'56 in this region. But it is certainly much more economical to have sufficient force to prevent a war between the Indians and whites than to suffer it to be created, thereby affording a pretext for volunteers to be called out by the territorial governors, and afterwards be obliged to bring the regular army into requisition to suppress it. The truth of this will be fully sustained when the bills for the services of the Oregon and Washington volunteers are rendered to Congress.

Eastern portion of Washington, and its connexion with the northwest portion of Nebraska, shown on map No. 21.

I have already referred to the importance of having six companies stationed in the valley of the Walla-Walla, and assigned, among other reasons, that of despatching two commands, consisting of two companies each, every year into the Indian country.

In chapter VI I have described the route to be followed in going from the Walla-Walla valley across the Blue mountains to Fort Boisé, on the Snake river. The routes which I shall now consider are marked A, B, C, on the map. Before describing these in detail, however, it will be well to consider somewhat the valley of the Walla-Walla river.

Fort Walla-Walla, situated at the junction of this river with the Columbia, was an old Hudson Bay Indian trading post. It was pillaged by the Indians in the war of the fall of 1855. It is now of no account, except to mark the miserable sandy spot where once it stood—as a place, among other purposes, used by explorers of the upper Columbia for rendezvous. From the mouth up the Walla-

Walla for 12 miles the banks are sandy and sterile. Ascending higher, however, we come to cottonwood and good land; and the valley, being cut up by many small streams, and having a mild climate, is inferior to none in the Territory for agricultural purposes. The whole country from this valley to the Snake river affords excellent grazing, and good timber grows in abundance at the headwaters and along the streams coming down from the Blue mountains.

Following the trail from the mouth up the river for about 20 miles we come to Mill creek, the present position of our military post, established by order of General Wool in 1856. The position is not far from where the treaty was held with the Indians by the superintendents of Indian affairs of Oregon and Washington, June, 1855, the practical fruits of which will be noticed more fully in another place.

ROUTE A.

From the mouth of the Walla-Walla to the mouth of the Snake river it is about 10 miles, following the bank of the Columbia, and the road is over a sandy soil, giving little difficulty in the passage. The Snake has to be crossed by boats. From its mouth the trail is on the Great Plain of the Columbia river for about 10 miles, when it strikes the Columbia river; from that point it bears a little east of north through a sandy district to a lake about six miles long and one mile wide, distant from the mouth of the Snake 62 miles. Following along this lake, and crossing a small feeder, the trail continues over the said Great Plain through a small coulée, from the northern extremity of which to the Grand Coulée it is 6 miles. The distance through the Grand Coulée is 20 miles. In it the soil is sandy, and there is a pond of good water. The northern extremity of this coulée is 10 miles wide; the southern is wider. Its walls are estimated at 800 feet in height, and consists of basaltic rock, seemingly cemented together with a kind of lava. On emerging we are immediately on the bank of the Columbia, at a distance of 140 miles from Old Fort Walla-Walla. On this whole extent not a tree occurs to relieve the eye from the continued monotony of grass and sand. On the southern part of the route, after leaving Snake river, the marches would be long between watering places, and there would be an insufficiency of grass for the animals of a train. Between the northern portion of this reach and the Columbia the country is full of coulées. From the northern extremity of the Grand Coulée the trail is on the east bank of the Columbia, through rough ground on the northern border of the Great Plain to the Spokane river, for a distance of 50 miles, on which timber and water are found. The Great Plain of the Columbia is but an extensive high table prairie. The mouth of the Spokane is is 200 feet wide, with a rapid current and a rocky bed. The banks are well timbered and the soil good. The crossing has to be made in canoes. From the Spokane, by the river trail, to Fort Colville, an old Hudson Bay Company Indian trading post, the distance is 50 miles, through a well wooded and well watered district; but without much labor it could not be rendered passable for wagons. The length of the route A, from Fort Walla to Fort Colville, is about 240 miles. It would not be a good route for troops to march over, nor would it be practicable for wagons beyond the Grand Coulée, except partially. Lieut. R. Arnold, 3d artillery, passed over this route with a small party in the last half of November, 1853. He does not report having met with any snow south of Fort Colville.

Distances on route A.

From—	To—	Miles.
Fort Walla-Walla	Whitman's Mission	25
Fort Walla-Walla	Mouth Snake river	10
Mouth Snake river	Columbia river	10
Columbia river	Lake	52
Lake	North extremity small coulée	42
North extremity small coulée	South extremity Grand Coulée	6
South extremity Grand Coulée	North extremity Grand Coulée	20
North extremity Grand Coulée	Spokane river	50
Spokane river	Fort Colville	50
Fort Walla-Walla	Fort Colville	240

ROUTE B.

This leads from the Walla-Walla valley, by the Pilouse river and over the Great Plain of the Columbia, to Fort Colville. From the Mission site, proceeding a little east of north to the Touchet river, it is about 18 miles, over a high rolling prairie bearing good grass and affording a tolerable passage for wagons. The Touchet is but a small tributary to the Walla-Walla. The valley is good for grazing and other farming purposes, and it is from one to two miles wide. There is an abundance of excellent pine building timber as we go up the stream towards the base of the Blue mountains.

From the Touchet to the mouth of the Pelouse—22 miles—it is a high rolling prairie of grass, but destitute of timber. The ascents and descents of the hills are easily made by winding along the slopes. The crossing of the Snake at the mouth of the Pelouse is difficult; it has to be made with boats, and the animals swim; it is 150 yards across, deep, rough, and rapid. The Snake has no valley here, and high hills on both sides come quite down to the water's edge. A rope scow-ferry could easily be arranged here. The valley of the Pelouse is well wooded, except for the first 10 miles above its mouth. The immediate valley and adjacent country are good for grazing. Should circumstances require it, this valley will afford a good military position.

From the mouth of the Pelouse—95 miles over the Great Plain to the Spokane—there is no timber. The plateau is generally high and rolling, of light soil, unfit for productive cultivation; grass is found on the least sandy parts. About 60 miles north of the Pelouse is a basaltic formation 24 miles wide, running east and west, which is the highest part of the plateau, much broken, and furnished with many little fresh water lakes.   Further north some willows and cottonwood fringe the streams in small patches.   Over the Great Plain on this route wagons can be passed without much difficulty from the 1st of June to the 15th of November.   A good stopping place can be had at Lake Sil-kat-ku.

The district of country embracing the lower part of the Spokane has plenty of timber, and excellent grazing and good water exist within accessible distances for animals sufficient for a large command. The mouth of this river is a great centre of Indian trails from all points of the compass, and there is an important fishery near by on the Columbia.   The lower portion of this river will afford a good position for a military post when the proper time will arrive for its use.   The stream is fordable where this route crosses it, except in very high stages.

From the Spokane to Fort Colville the scene changes materially from that presented to the south.   After passing through a scattering wood for five miles we ascend the Che-ma-kane river to its head waters in a low mountain range; crossing this divide the trail descends the valley of the Slawn-te-hus river.   This valley is thirty-five miles long by one or two in width; the soil is generally quite good, and there are some settlements in it; the banks are subject to overflow; the stream is fordable in summer.   The dividing ridge is timbered, and no difficulty is in the way of making a good wagon road along these two streams and across this divide.   At present, from the Spokane 60 miles to Fort Colville, pack trains only can pass, and even these should not attempt to pass before the 1st of June.

Fort Colville would be a first rate point to occupy with troops in reference to British Indians to the north.   Owing to the existence of gold, which attracts so many to 'this place, and who seem to be increasing every season in numbers, the War Department should not be surprised soon to find it necessary to send a command into this region, more for the purpose of preventing outrages upon the Indians than from them.   The mountain trails from various parts centering at the fort are practicable for pack animal trains in summer.

Distances on B. and other routes.

From—	To—	Miles.
Fort Walla-Walla	Mouth of the Pelouse	50
Whitman's Mission	Touchet river	18
Touchet river	Mouth of Pelouse	22
Mouth of Pelouse	Lake Sil-kat-ku	45
Lake Sil-kat-ku	Spokane river	50
Spokane river	Summit of mountains	22
Summit of mountains	Fort Colville	38
Fort Colville	Osoycos lake	66
Fort Colville	Mouth of Clark's Fork	35
Fort Colville	Pend d'Oreille lake	90
Spokane river	Pend d'Oreille lake	70
Spokane river	Coeur d'Alene	36

Navigability of the Columbia, between Forts Walla-Walla and Colville.

As I have referred to the fact of there being good sites, in case of a necessity for their use, for military posts on the Pelouse and the Spokane, the question naturally arises as to the advantage that can be taken of the Columbia for the purposes of transportation. This puts me to the task of giving some reliable information on the navigability of the upper Columbia.

Between Forts Walla-Walla and Colville three serious obstacles occur, viz: Priest's rapids, approximatively located 60 miles above Fort Walla-Walla; Buckland's rapids, 66 miles higher up; and Kettle falls, 296 miles still higher up, which are just below Fort Colville. Around all three portages would have to be made. These natural barriers, as in other rivers, serve to divide the stream into pools or reaches, which are navigable for light draught boats and canoes. But in regard to the sand bars, shoals, deposits, snags, sawyers, sunken rocks, and swift places, which might be hindrances, nothing is known from which we can form an estimate of any reliability. George Suckley, esq., late assistant surgeon United States army, descended the Columbia from Fort Colville in a canoe, (four persons,) leaving November 17 and arriving at Fort Walla-Walla December 1, 1853. He is of the opinion, derived from his own observations during this descent, that in these reaches or pools a steamer drawing from 20 to 30 inches could navigate in low stages of the river. The average speed of his canoe was $3\frac{2}{3}$ miles per hour. This does not indicate a very swift current. He does not report having encountered snow or ice.

Between Fort Walla-Walla and the mouth of the Spokane only two of the named obstructions occur. Ross and Thompson's rapids (located from Wilkes' map) are regarded by Dr. Suckley as affording no material obstacle to steam navigation. There is no timber whatever growing on the banks of the Columbia between a point 34 miles below the mouth of the Spokane and Fort Dalles, which is 115 miles below Fort Walla-Walla. Above Fort Colville Lieutenant Arnold, 3d artillery, made an examination to a point $3\frac{1}{2}$ miles above the mouth of Clark's Fork in the first part of November, 1853. He reports the current swift, and numerous small rapids; his canoes were four days ascending 25 miles. Clark's Fork enters at a point very near the 49th parallel, which is the boundary between us and the British, if not exactly on it. This fork debouches through a mountain gorge, which is a short distance above its mouth, where there is a fall of 3 feet, and directly at the mouth there is a fall of 15 feet. These preclude the idea of ascending the lower part of this stream by boats. I submit the following table of distances, prepared from the best data obtainable until actual surveys shall be made of the upper Columbia, confining my table to the portion within our own possessions—that is, from its mouth to the 49th parallel of north latitude:

Navigable reaches of the Columbia.

From—	To—	Miles.
Mouth of Columbia	Foot of Cascades	183
Head of Cascades	Foot of the Dalles	45
Head of the Des Chutes	Foot of Priest's rapids	160
Head of Buckland's rapids	Foot of Kettle's falls	66
Head of Kettle's falls	Foot of Little Dalles	296
Head of Little Dalles	49th parallel, Clark's Fork	33

The aggregate of all the portages would be about 25 miles in length. Hence the total approximate length of this river within our own possessions is 818 miles. The first two named reaches are now successfully navigated with steamers. A portion of the reach— from Des Chutes up to Walla-Walla, 100 miles—is now being used for transporting supplies in oar-boats for the post on Mill creek. The results of this experiment have not yet been given sufficiently in detail to determine the saving of this mode of overland transportation between Fort Dalles and that post.

I by no means regard the problem of the navigability of the Columbia above Fort Dalles, for military purposes, as having yet been solved. What I have here given in a condensed form embodies all that we know pertinent to this interesting question; nor can the problem be solved except by results from proper surveys of the pools, portages, rapids, &c., under a competent officer, with ample funds for the purpose. The sum of $25,000, with orders for the troops to afford protection, would be required for the accomplishment of the object.

ROUTE C.

From the Walla-Walla, via Cœur d'Alene, thence to Fort Benton, on the Missouri river, in Nebraska.

From the treaty ground to Snake river, 61 miles, it is a rolling prairie, with cottonwood on the banks of the streams; there are plentiful supplies of water and grass for any number of animals; the streams are easily crossed, and it is a good district for dragoons or infantry to operate in. The Snake has to be crossed by boats. It is here that we come to the Nez Percés Indian country, and this is known as "Red Wolf Crossing." The banks of the river are low. The creeks in the vicinity are well wooded.

From the Snake to the Pelouse river, 39 miles, it is a prairie easy of passage; it grows the camas, indicating a moist, rich soil. The valley of the Pelouse is well filled with good pine timber, and the stream is fordable in summer.

From the Pelouse, 50 miles to the Cœur d'Alene river, the passage generally is easy, the country well wooded, and water and grass are met in abundance. There is, however, a range of hills to cross where it would be difficult for a wagon to pass without labor, just south of Nedlehualk creek; and a mountain to cross before reaching St. Joseph river, requiring considerable work to make the road good for loaded wagons. After this, there is a lake that would have to be bridged. There is plenty of timber on the spot to bridge wherever required in this reach. The Cœur d'Alene is easily bridged. Any number of animals may be grazed all the way from the starting point on this route for 123 miles, to near the mountain just mentioned.

From the crossing of the Cœur d'Alene river, *via* the Mission, to the foot of the Cœur d'Alene mountain pass, it is 60 miles, following the north trail seen on the map as we cross the mountain. In this long reach there is much timber, through which, however, a good wagon road could be made with little difficulty, except for six or seven miles, where the trail is seen to bend away from the river before reaching the entrance of the pass. This pass is only $4\frac{1}{2}$ miles through from stream to stream. In it there is a steep hill to go over; it is heavily timbered, requiring much labor in cutting fallen timber and in side-hill digging, to make a tolerable road through it, and probably some rock blasting would be required.

From the east extremity of said pass to Hell Gate it is 106 miles, in which there are two difficult places to make a road through: one, marked *a*, between where the trail leaves the St. Regia Borgia and the Bitter Root river, 13 miles in extent; the other, marked *b*, 20 miles long, in which blasting would be necessary in several places. Possibly a better route for a road could be found through the timbered bottom on the south side of the stream.

From Hell Gate to the west foot of Cadott's Pass, in the Rocky mountains, it is 89 miles, and there would be no serious difficulty in making a wagon road. In the valleys of the Hell Gate and St. Mary's rivers any number of animals could be grazed all summer. There is a great deal of prairie as well as timber land in these, also in that of the Blackfoot Fork. Through Cadott's Pass, for 26 miles, I estimate that two companies of troops could open a good wagon road in 10 days; the ridge is very steep and much work would be required.

We have now come to the boundary between Washington and Nebraska, and from the west extremity of the pass it is 133 miles to Fort Benton; between the foot of the pass on the east side to the fort, there is very little in the way of the passage of a wagon train.

I have mentioned the difficulties in the way of moving a wagon train over the whole route. In the present condition of the trail starting by the 15th June, with one or two companies of dragoons, and plenty of pack animals, the whole march from the treaty ground in the valley of the Walla-Walla (543 miles) to Fort Benton could be performed in 32 days, and from the treaty ground (250 miles) to the Bitter Root river in 22 days. Grass would be found sufficient for the subsistence of mules and Indian horses. But if American horses be used, they should be accustomed for two seasons to live on the grass before starting. The only streams to be ferried or swam would be the Snake, Pown lake, Cœur d'Alene river, Bitter Root, and the Hell Gate—all the others would be found fordable. Pown lake could be avoided by diverging, so as to cross the Cœur d'Alene river below Cœur d'Alene lake, but it would increase the distance 35 miles.

Returning the same year from Fort Benton to the Walla-Walla valley with the same command, the circumstances would be different. On this point we have the data of Governor Stevens' return trip in the fall of 1855. Leaving Fort Benton 5th November, his travelling time continued to 20th December, but his party were under march only 36 days. It was a very cold season, snows had commenced to fall at Fort Benton on the day of starting, and it was found in Cadott's Pass, on the Cœur d'Alene mountains, at the Clear Water river, and in the Walla-Walla valley, where the party arrived 20th December. The Columbia had frozen over that same season, and there were deep snows on the trails in the Yakama country in November. The animals of the party were worn down and much distressed for the want of sufficient grass, many were exchanged for others on the route in trade with the Indians.

I regard the route C the best, all circumstances considered, for opening a wagon road upon, between our military post in the valley of the Walla-Walla and Fort Benton. It combines more advantages than any other route; the total distance is 543 miles. After arriving at the Pelouse, for the whole of the remaining distance this route is common with that designated by the late Secretary of War, Jefferson Davis, for the 4th regiment of infantry to open a wagon road upon during an overland march from Walla-Walla. to Fort Benton. It is quite certain the road, if opened, would seldom, if ever, be used by emigrants to the Pacific; its principal use would be for military purposes, and in this point of view it would be of some importance in affording communication between the departments of the west and Pacific, if the road were well opened and afterwards kept in repair. It would also serve the desirable end of connecting, as it were, the valleys of the Walla-Walla, Cœur d'Alene, and St. Mary's, each of which being well adapted to the growing of stock and agricultural products, and possessing good climate and an abundance of good water, may, in time, be coveted for settlement by the whites. These valleys, however, afford no more than is needed by the Indians, who occupy them. To construct the road by the labor of a regiment of troops, as contemplated in the orders of the late honorable Secretary, would require two to three years in the field, and it would cost vastly more than to do it by contract, under a special appropriation. The proper use of troops, in connexion with such an undertaking, would be to perform escort duty, and to protect the laboring parties against the Indians.

With such aid from the troops, and an appropriation of $350,000, the road could probably be opened all the way, and the necessary bridges constructed, and the whole line put in such condition that a team could haul a reasonable load over it at the usual rate of teaming on a pretty fair country road. But, after being put in this condition, annual repairs must be made upon it, or else in two years it would be found impassable in many places.

Distances on route C.

From—	To—	Miles.
Treaty ground, (Mill creek)	Touchet river	23
Touchet river	Toutañon creek	16
Toutañon creek	Snake river	22
Snake river	Pelouse river	39
Pelouse river	Nedlehualk creek	18
Nedlehualk creek	St. Joseph river	20
St. Joseph river	Cœur d'Alene river	12
Cœur d'Alene river	Cœur d'Alene Mission	15
Cœur d'Alene Mission	Fork of trails	29
Fork of trails	West foot Northern Pass	16
West foot Cœur d'Alene Pass	East foot of pass	4½
East foot of pass	Junction of trails	5
Junction of trails	Leaving St. Regia river	18
Leaving St. Regia river	Bitter Root river	13
Military post, Walla-Walla valley	Bitter Root river	250
Bitter Root river	Hell Gate	70
East foot Cœur d'Alene Pass	Hell Gate	106
Hell Gate	West foot Cadott's Pass	89
West foot Cadott's Pass	East foot Cadott's Pass	26
East foot Cadott's Pass	Fort Benton	107
Military post, Mill creek, Walla-Walla.	Fort Benton	543

VIII. *Indian treaties and their effects in Washington Territory.*

Ascending the Columbia for about 75 miles above Fort Dalles (map 20) we reach the mouth of the Umatilla, which, coming from the east, drains a valley occupied by the Umatilla tribe.

Higher up, at a distance of about 120 miles above the fort, is the mouth of the Walla-Walla river, which drains a district east of the Columbia and south of the Snake river, (Lewis's Fork of the Columbia.) This district is the home of the Walla-Walla tribe. It also contains that of the Cayuses, who, however, occupy the portion towards the Blue mountains, while the former occupy that nearer the Columbia and the Snake.

Ascending the Columbia still higher, for about twenty miles above the mouth of the Walla-Walla, we come to the mouth of the Yakama river, which, with its tributaries, drains a large district to the north and west of the Columbia, belonging to the Yakama tribe, (maps 17, 20.)

The Snake river enters the Columbia between the mouths of the Walla-Walla and the Yakama about ten miles below the latter. The localities are readily comprehended by observing, at a few miles below the entrance of the Walla-Walla, the Columbia makes a right angle in its course; down to this elbow it comes from the north, and below its course is westerly to the Pacific.

Ascending the Snake river 130 miles above its mouth, we come to the Koos-koos-ky river, (map 21.) To the south of this and to the east of the Snake is the Nez Percé Indian country.

On the 29th May, 1855, the superintendents of Indian affairs (Stevens and Palmer) for Washington and Oregon, as commissioners on the part of the United States, met the assembled tribes above named, and others of lesser note, for a council, at the treaty ground already mentioned, on Mill creek, in the valley of the Walla-Walla. About eight tribes, with their chiefs and headmen, were present. The whole number was about 5,000 ; at the sittings of the council, however, there were present only about 1,000.

The *tout ensemble* of each tribe, on this occasion, was magnificence in the extreme; while that of the whites, on the contrary, was meagre and insignificant. It was humiliating to witness the contrast, so unfavorable to the success so earnestly hoped for. The Indians, as they advanced in bodies of from three to twelve hundred warriors from their distant homes, were all mounted upon fine horses, having their equipments, though of Indian taste, most richly and gorgeously ornamented. The riders strode their steeds with grace and skill. Not so with the whites ; the retinue of the commissioners was shabby, diminutive, and mean in appointments generally, and deficient in all those points of show, in particular, that are so well calculated to strike the fancy or command the respect of an Indian. The pitiful escort of the commissioners of only thirty to forty United States infantry soldiers, mounted on lame, gaunt horses and mules, literally fed on nothing, furnished by the quartermaster at the Dalles the previous winter, and having no show in equipments, nor riders possessing skill in horsemanship—this escort, we say, contrasted most unfortunately with the splendid array presented by 1,200 Nez Percé horsemen. In short, there was not a tribe that did not outnumber, outshine, and outdo the whites in all those points so well calculated, and which should never be disregarded, to produce a favorable effect on the savage mind when assembled in council. To argue the opposite of this would be tantamount to confessing ignorance of the Indian character.

By allowing themselves to go into council under such circumstances the commissioners, at the outset, jeopardized the very object of the nogotiation. Even the Cayuses, the smallest in numbers, manifested utter contempt for the military escort, and their young braves even dared to turn the cold shoulder to the young officer commanding the paltry troop of infantry. On such an occasion, when so much was pending, there should have been four full companies of dragoons at least, well mounted and fully uniformed and equipped. The prudence of the officer at the critical moment is to be commended; his cool personal daring saved him; had he attempted to rely on his handful of soldiers to avenge the insult, probably every white man of the embassy would have been made to bite the dust. Your escort at a grand council of assembled tribes should be able to outdo the Indians if you expect them to be impressed with a sense of your superiority; otherwise the moral effect is all against you. If the United States' troops at the Dalles and Vancouver had not so early as May "emerged from the lethargy of winter quarters," or were too few or deficient in kind to afford a suitable escort, surely, in virtue of his gubernatorial power, one of the commissioners could have commanded the attendance of four companies of Washington mounted volunteers; or

H. Ex. Doc. 114——6

perchance the paucity of numbers in that Territory not furnishing that force, then his brother governor, of the adjacent Territory, would unquestionably have accommodated him with a battalion of Oregon volunteers. Be this as it may, it is difficult to resist the conclusion that, in military preparations, there was an oversight little to have been expected in the chief of the embassy, considering his military antecedents. We are willing, however, to believe that he was not alone to blame, and that an obstacle was interposed by the Secretary of War declining to authorize a sufficient military escort from the United States troops, on the ground of a deficiency of numbers then in the department. There may have been another reason for denying a suitable escort, which may be attributed to that unfortunate jealously, or something worse, existing between the Indian Bureau and War Department, the fruits of which are most pernicious. To the effects of this want of unity I shall more particularly refer in another place.

The object principally designed in assembling these tribes in a grand council was, to engage them to abandon the lands upon which they had been born, and grazed their herds of cattle and horses, and lived and hunted; to quit forever the streams on which their canoes had been paddled by their squaws and children, and in which they had fished for the salmon from a period long antecedent to the descent of Lewis and Clark; and to exchange all their possessory rights to the soil of extensive tracts over which they had roamed for many a generation in undisputed dominion for other more circumscribed lands called "Indian reservation," which were to be designated and agreed upon in council.

It cannot be denied that the object of the whites in holding this treaty was one of grave import, involving the future destiny of no less than five tribes of intelligent, warlike, well armed, and well appointed savages, all of which tribes, except one, (the Cayuses,) had been on friendly terms with the whites up to the meeting of this council; and one of them, the Walla-Walla, headed by their distinguished chief, the late Pee-pee-mox-mox, had done good service in battle in aid of the conquest of California—a service not readily forgotten by those engaged in that enterprise.

Neither is it to be denied that the Indians may have had some general ideas of the objects of assembling them, though previously to the opening of the council it is not to be doubted their ideas of the principal object in view were exceedingly vague and indefinite. The tribes were undoubtedly stimulated with the prospect that the commissioners would come loaded with numerous fine Indian goods and much money to distribute among them. It was more from a desire to become the recipients of these as gifts than from any other influence that they allowed themselves to be assembled. Very far was it from the intention of their chiefs to relinquish or exchange one square rod of their lands upon any consideration whatever.

Proceedings of the council.—The sessions commenced May 29 and terminated June 11, occasionally adjourning over one day to allow time to digest what had been said previously.

Unmistakable repugnance to the treaty was evinced throughout, not only by the chiefs, but by the individuals composing the tribes, almost to a man. Lawyer, the head chief of the Nez Percés, was the first to apparently give in to the views of the commissioners, but not until the tenth day of the sessions; and then he had the boldness to couple his sanction with expressing his want of confidence in the fulfilment of the brilliant promises held up to his people by the commissioners, twitting them with a breach on the part of the whites in non-complying with a former treaty.

The Cayuse chiefs were strongly opposed to the terms proposed, alleging they had no right to sell the ground God had given for the support of the Indians, except for good reasons, and that they could not clearly see the things promised on the part of the whites as compensation.

Pee-pee-mox-mox and Five Crows, chiefs of the Walla-Wallas, opposed the treaty. The former urged strongly upon the commissioners the bad effect of bringing a treaty like this to a hasty conclusion; he plead for more time for his people to consider it, and offered to meet the commissioners in another council, if their Great Father (the President) should desire it after knowing the sentiments of his red subjects against removing from their lands; and he would give the commissioners one day to consider his proposition.

Kameakin and Schloom, chiefs of the Yakamas, were so indignant at the object proposed that they would not speak in council when invited, except to say " we have nothing to say."

Ow-hi, for the Umatillas, acknowledged his obligation to the Great Spirit, and to no one else, for the right of the Indians to the soil they occupied, and refused to steal it away from his people by selling it, as the commissioners proposed, to the whites.

Up to the tenth session all the chiefs, except Lawyer, strongly and openly opposed the treaty; and one knowing this crafty old chief could easily perceive he was playing a game diplomatique, and whatever his hand might do in the making of his mark on a piece of paper, his heart was opposed to its contents. So strong was the opposition of the chiefs in council, of those outside, and of the tribes collectively and individually, that on the eleventh session the commissioners receded in some measure from their first demands and essentially modified the treaty. To this modification they gained, apparently, the reluctant assent of all the chiefs then present in council, except those of the Yakama tribe; and, with this exception, all seemed going on well until, just before adjournment on this same day, Looking-Glass, the great war chief of the Nez Percés, (who up to this time had not been present,) made his appearance on the ground—first sending a runner to herald his approach—escorted by a well mounted war band, and, before dismounting, denounced to the superintendent for Washington the selling of the Nez Percé country to the whites. It is to be observed this chief, though second in rank to Lawyer, has much influence with the people of this tribe.

The next day the senior commissioner opened the proceedings in a speech, in which he labored most assiduously to convince Looking-Glass, who was now seated in council, of the advantages to his people and to himself held out in the treaty, in which it was demanded that there were "to be three reservations, one upon which the Cayuses, the Walla-Wallas, and the Umatillas were to go; one upon which the Nez Percés were to be placed, and one upon which the Yakamas were to be confined; and that they were to be removed from their present possessions to these reservations in the course of two or three years."

To this, Looking-Glass immediately rose, and, in a well set speech, replied against the policy of the treaty, and with such an effect that all the chiefs, Lawyer inclusive, refused to submit to it. Both commissioners rejoined at length, urging him to change his decision; convinced that, unless Looking-Glass were gained over, all would be lost; but their arguments in council were in vain, and it was in this state of the proceedings when the council was adjourned over Sunday (that being a religious day with the Nez Percés) to meet again on Monday.

On Monday, June 11, the senior commissioner opened the council with a brief address, at the close of which, on invitation from his excellency, all the chiefs came forward and signed the treaty, apparently without opposition. After which, the presents were distributed to the chiefs, and the council was dissolved; the superintendent for Washington leaving, with an escort only of Nez Percés, for Fort Benton, 543 miles distant, to hold another treaty; the superintendent for Oregon leaving for Port Orford, to hold the treaty spoken of in chapter VI, on Rogue river; the mounted troop of forty infantry returning to Fort Dalles, their further services as escort being ended, and the tribes were dismissed to their several homes.

The questions naturally arise, how and by what means, during that adjournment over Sunday, were the chiefs operated upon to induce them to sign a treaty to which the commissioners knew all, except Lawyer, were so violently opposed? What potential consideration was brought to bear with such talismanic effect as to cause so wonderful a change in the dispositions of the chiefs? What was it that had more influence on the savage mind, during that adjournment, than all the speeches the commissioners had made during the eleven previous days? Let the commissioners answer. We go on to adduce some of the effects of their diplomacy.

There is little doubt that Lawyer and Looking-Glass had a previous understanding that the former was to cajole the commissioners to believe him favorably disposed to their views; and, in the nick of time, Looking-Glass was to appear, as he did, suddenly on the ground, and oppose the negotiation; this for the double purpose of making the whites believe in the friendliness of the Nez Percés, and at the same time to throw obstacles in the way to prevent a clutch upon their lands from being realized. In these respects, events have shown that the crafty Lawyer was the ablest diplomatist at the council; for the friendship of his tribe has remained, and no hold upon their lands has yet inured to the whites.

No disinterested witness to the proceedings believed that a single chief signed that treaty with the slightest possible intention of abiding it. They all regarded it as a paper to which they affixed their marks without their hearts being with their hands; and the commissioners, in their cool and rational moments, ought to have known there was no intention on the part of the tribes to fulfil its stipulations; and they also ought to have known that all the tribes (except, perhaps, the Nez Percé) left the council ground with feelings much less friendly than they entertained before being summoned to this council. Were these commissioners so heated by the anxious desire of fame in the diplomatique field as to have been blinded to the fact that it was a question among the tribes whether they would not then rise in arms upon the commissioners' party and seize all the goods they had brought, and that the scheme was not executed was owing to the policy of old Lawyer?

The effects of the Walla-Walla treaty are summed up as follows :

1. The meagre escort and shabby appearance of the commission created in the minds of the warriors an idea of military weakness on the part of the whites; and this was helped to be confirmed in their minds by the fact that a band of Cayuses, eight years previous, had gained a decided victory in an open field fight over a battalion of mounted Oregonians, in equal numbers to the Indians, but quadruple the infantry escort at the council.

2. The refusal to allow time, as urged by Pee-pee-mox-mox, for individuals of the tribes to consider the proposition of moving from their father lands to new homes, convinced the Indians that they were to go or not to go, to be or not to be, at the pleasure of the whites, and that the wishes, conveniences, or welfare of the Indians were but as dust in the balance.

3. The small number, small size, and allotment of the reservations, viz : one for the Nez Percés, one for the Yakamas, and only one upon which all the other tribes and fractions were to be condensed, created a perception of the want of fairness and liberality on the part of the commissioners. It is not to be supposed six tribes of Indians could have been contented within the limits of one reservation, without just apprehension of serious collision among themselves, which even they would have good reason to dread.

4. The manner in which the head chiefs were ultimately brought over to sign the treaty was calculated to cause discontent in the minds of all less favored in the tribes—necessarily begetting dissatis-faction, engendering opposition, and determination to disregard what the favored chiefs had signed.

5. The hot haste and grasping disposition evinced by the senior commissioner in his speeches in council, and, as shown by the terms of the treaty, requiring in so short a time the relinquishment of so much country of their birthright, and the threatening argument that, if they did not leave their lands, the whites would come and take them, must necessarily have produced bitter feelings, akin to despair, or a resolution to defend those rights to the last.

6. The marked preference shown in the selection of the body of the Nes Percés for an escort to Fort Benton was calculated to produce envy in the minds of the other less favored tribes; and yet, if Indians were to be employed for military service, it will be conceded by all

acquainted with the Nez Percés that a better band could not have been chosen for a body guard on this occasion.

7. The recollection, still operating in the minds of some of the tribes at this council, of a breach of faith on the part of the whites, in reference to a treaty negotiated on a former occasion, was sufficient to teach that if a treaty was broken by the whites, with equal fairness one could be disregarded by the Indians; and hence their opinion that the mere act of signing a treaty was not necessarily to be regarded as binding themselves to execute it; and when afterwards informed that a failure to comply with its conditions would bring the armed vengeance of the whites upon them, it is not surprising that they regarded this an additional bitterness poured into their cup, already full to overflowing.

We now perceive how it was that the hearts and minds of these tribes were wrought up to a pitch of desperate determination to resist, being, as they thought, driven or cheated into the scheme of despoliation of their lands. And here we perceive the chief if not the primary cause of all these tribes, except the Nez Percés, joining in a war commenced in the Yakama country only three months after the dissolution of this council.

Quitting the council ground, as stated, for Fort Benton, the superintendent for Washington left in his rear a vast extent of Indian country, in which the proceedings of the council had stirred up little else than strong dissatisfaction in the Indian heart; advancing so far into an Indian country, leaving the country behind upon the point of blazing into open hostilities, and pursuing his way without an adequate escort of United States troops seems surprising; it certainly was an act which, though a bold one, cannot be too strongly condemned. What effect could it have but that of an exhibition of military weakness on the part of the whites?

Gold had been discovered by some "half-breeds" in the neighborhood of Fort Colville, high up on the Columbia, and the announcement of it was made about the time of holding this council. As is usual on such events, hundreds of whites went flocking to the auriferous district. The rush commenced soon after the close of the council. The routes thither led directly through the Walla-Walla and Yakama countries, and as the whites passed, some of them committed excesses and outrages of the grossest kinds upon the hitherto unoffending Indians of the very tribes the proceedings of the council had so much and so recently disturbed. The bare recital of some of the crimes committed by these Anglo-Saxon devils, in human shape, is sufficient to cause the blood of every virtuous man, whether of red or white skin, to boil with deep indignation. They were not satisfied with stealing the horses and cattle of the Indians, but they claimed the privilege of taking and ravishing Indian women and maidens *ad libitum*. What wonder, then, that the Indians who had been so grossly outraged should have retaliated, as they did, by killing some half dozen of these miscreants?

Sub-Indian Agent Bolon, yet swelling with the importance he had acquired by the part he had played at the recent council, threatened the Indians who had retaliated, as described, with the vengeance of the United States government, and actually started on his way, and told the Indians he was going to Fort Dalles to fetch the troops against them. Whether this was a mere threat, meant to frighten the Indians, is not known. Be this as it may, they believed him in earnest. Three of their number followed, and overtaking him, demanded to know if he intended to send the United States troops against them? On answering in the affirmative, as the Indians say, they killed him, and afterwards, as reported, some miners on their way to Colville.

However much we may regret the death of Mr. Bolon by the savage hand, it cannot be denied his own gross imprudence, in threatening the Indians with a hostile visit of the United States troops, was more the cause of his death than any prejudice or ill will against him. It was an act committed, probably, to save themselves from chastisement at the hands of the troops. These views on the subject under consideration were formed in the month of November, 1855, two months after the occurrence, while engaged in a reconnaissance in that portion of the country. They are the results of my own investigation at that time into the first causes of the hostilities commenced there in October. I have not officially reported these views until now, having preferred to wait for such additional evidence as naturally would be subsequently developed calculated either to confirm or refute them. From all l ghts I have since, from time to time, been able to obtain, I am more and more convinced of their correctness.

Colonel Wright, 9th infantry, in command, reports from his camp on the Nachess river, Yakama country, (map 17,) May 30, 1856, and says: "I believe most of these chiefs desire peace, but some of them hold back in fear of the demands that may be made upon them for their murders and thefts. They seem to think and say that they had strong and good reasons for the murders they have committed, both of the miners and Indian agent, (Bolon;) the outrages of the former and the injudicious and intemperate threats of the latter, if true, as they say, I doubt not maddened the Indians to murder them."

I have given what I regard as the causes of and acts immediately preceding the Indian war in Oregon and Washington in 1855-'56. It was at the time clearly shown to my own mind, by my own investigations of facts, that the principal cause is to be found in what I have stated in reference to the Walla-Walla council and the treaty there made.

Since that war commenced, I know it has been said by those holding high positions that it was one determined upon, a long time previous to the council, in a secret combination of tribes resolved upon exterminating the whites; but upon examination of this opinion, whenever and by whomsoever expressed, I find it to rest on *ipse dixits*, mere sayings without proof. In the annual report of the Secretary of War, December 1, 1856, it is said: "A combination embracing most of the tribes inhabiting those Territories (Washington and Oregon) was entered into, and the extermination of the whites seemed to be their purpose." This is a most comprehensive charge against the very many tribes occupying those Territories, and it comes from high authority. But I have hunted in vain for credible evidence to substantiate it to the extent of its declaration. I think the Hon. Secretary may have forgotten the number of tribes in those Territories.

On the 11th June, 1856, Colonel Wright reports from his camp on the Nachess: "The chiefs all sent the most friendly messages. I answered, they must come and see me. Ow-hi and Te-vi-as came, and we had a long talk about the war, its origin, &c. Ow-hi related the whole history of the Walla-Walla treaty, and concluded by saying that the war commenced from that moment—that the treaty was the cause of all the deaths by fighting since that time. Ow-hi is a very intelligent man. He speaks with great energy, is well acquainted with his subject, and his words carry conviction of truth to his hearers." Ow-hi, though a Yakama chief, it will be remembered, spoke at that council for the Umatillas; his speech not only conveyed the sentiments of his tribe, but it was likewise an index to the minds of his own people.

It is not to be doubted that during the council some of the chiefs were secretly plotting. The occasion afforded them too good an opportunity to be lost for talking over their grievances and concocting plans. In this sense, it may be, there was a combination of some of the eight bands assembled.

Is it to be presumed the commissioners were not aware of the temper in which they left those Indians? Is it to be believed they were cajoled into the idea that the chiefs meant to comply with the stipulations? It would be passing but a poor compliment upon the discernment of the President's ambassadors to answer those interrogations affirmatively.

Was it not, then, the duty of these gentlemen to immediately inform the military commander of the department of the bad temper existing among them? Instead of which, on the contrary, one of the commissioners, soon after coming from the council, sent a message to General Wool, assuring him all was quiet there; that the Indians attending the council were all friendly disposed, and that happy results were anticipated immediately to flow in consequence of the treaty. This message was communicated to the general at his headquarters about the 1st September, and it was the only communication to him, direct or indirect, after the holding of the council, from either commissioner on the subject until the war commenced.

The commanding general of the department had returned from his inspection of the posts on the Columbia in the preceding June, after organizing and sending a command from Fort Dalles into the Fort Boisé district, under Brevet Major Haller, 4th infantry, as explained under the head of "Eastern Oregon," and had then left all peaceful in the whole of Washington Territory, as well as in Oregon. Major Haller's command returned to Fort Dalles about the last of September with his animals much worn down after so long a march.

IX. *Military operations during the Indian war of 1855–'56, in Washington and Northern Oregon.*

In chapter VIII the cause of this war has been given. In this chapter I shall record the procedings and operations of the troops, regulars and volunteers, as briefly as consistent with a clear narrative of the principal circumstances.

Up to the time of the murder of Sub-Indian Agent Bolon, in September, 1855, there were only three military posts in all this country, viz: Fort Steilacoom, garrisoned with two companies 4th infantry; Fort Vancouver, with two companies 4th infantry and on ecompany 3d artillery; Fort Dalles, with two companies 4th infantry and a small detachment of dragoons; the troops at the latter post having, as before stated, quite recently returned from the Snake River expedition, were under the immediate command of Captain (Brevet Major) Haller. Major G. J. Rains, then commanding the 4th regiment infantry, was the senior officer in all these districts, with his headquarters at Fort Vancouver.

On being informed of the murder of Sub-Agent Bolon, and on a call upon him for troops by the then acting Governor Mason, of Washington, Major Rains reports, 3d of October, 1855: "We have sent 40 men with two officers from Fort Steilacoom, and 102 men with five officers from Fort Dalles, into the Yakama country, and shall follow, if necessary, with all our force."

Here it will be seen that the call from the acting governor (in the absence of Governor Stevens, who was then on the Missouri, about 1,000 miles distant from Olympia) upon the army for troops was most promptly met by Major Rains.

At this time General Wool, commanding the department of the Pacific, was at his headquarters, Benicia, California, more than 1,000 miles distant from the scene of threatened hostilities. It is here to be observed that the only direct means of communicating from Fort Vancouver to his headquarters was by the semi-monthly sea steamer, whose trips were so regulated that she arrived at San Francisco on or about the 4th and 19th of every month; and as in good weather she required five to six days to make the run, she would leave Portland, bringing despatches from the Columbia river, about the 29th of one month and the 13th of the following month. These despatches could only reach the general on the nights of the 5th or 6th and 19th or 20th of each month. And in transmitting despatches from his headquarters, they had to leave Benicia not later than the 4th and 19th to reach the Columbia river and Puget's Sound posts. I have put in this explanation to show how it was that information of Major Rains' action, October 9, calling for volunteers, did not reach General Wool until the 19th of the same month.

The little force under Lieutenant Slaughter, from Fort Steilacoom, was to proceed through the Nachess Pass, (maps 16 and 17,) and that from Fort Dalles, under Major Haller, by the route seen on map 19, into the Yakama country. The former started and was far on its way

when, learning of the Indian force in front, it judiciously returned to
White river.   On the afternoon of October 6 Major Haller's command
fell in with the Indians, and commenced an action with them in the
brush on the Pisco river, and, after fighting some time, drove them at
the point of the bayonet, and took possession of a hill; he was surrounded by Indians, and called for a reinforcement.   This call reached
Major Rains on the 9th, and the next day Lieutenant Day, 4th artillery,
started from Fort Dalles with 45 men and a mountain howitzer to
reinforce Major Haller.

Major Rains reports the same day, October 9, to the governor of
Oregon, and says: "As commanding officer, I have ordered all the
United States disposable force in this district into the field immediately, and shall take command.   As this force is questionable to
subdue these Indians—the Yakamas, Klikatats, and may be some other
smaller bands—I have the honor to call upon you for four companies of
volunteers, composed according to our present organization.   This is
just enough for a Major's command, and would authorize that officer
also.   They can be mustered here, (at Fort Vancouver)."

Such was the call for Oregon volunteers, made by Major Rains, by
what authority it doth not appear, except perhaps from what he
derived in virtue of having assumed, being "commanding officer;"
it will be perceived there were only four companies called for, and they
were intended by Major Rains to be mustered into the United States
service at Fort Vancouver.

Whether there was any real necessity for such an additional force
to Major Rains' command I will not pretend to decide, but that the
call for these volunteers proved an embarrassment to him there can
be no doubt.   After events must have convinced him that his call
was turned to a very different end from what he contemplated.

On the 10th October Major Haller's command, after much hard
fighting, succeeded in retreating to Fort Dalles, with severe loss in
killed and wounded, in pack animals and one howitzer.   The field is
marked on maps 17–19.   It was a brave fight, in retreat gallantly
covered by Captain Russell's company.

Major Rains says in his remarkable official address (13th November, 1855) to the Yakama Indians: "I sent this handful of soldiers
into your country to inquire into the facts of the murder of Indian
Agent Bolon; it was not expected that they should fight you."   From
this it would seem that Major Haller attacked the Yakamas without
authority of his commanding officer.

The effect of this defeat—for such it must be considered—was to
embolden the Indians on the immediate east of the Cascade range;
and the news of it spreading like wild-fire, extended through the passes
to the Indians west of it, even to the Puget's Sound district; to the
east it went with equal celerity across the Columbia to the Walla-
Wallas, Spokanes, &c.

As before said, and for the reasons assigned, the commanding general of the department did not receive until the 19th October information of events that had occurred in the order related up to the
13th October.   The action of the governor of Oregon upon Major

Rains call for volunteers was not made known until after the steamer left Portland.

On the 19th October the general ordered two detachments—one from Benicia, the other from Presidio, composed of 1 captain, (Ord,) 2 lieutenants, and 70 rank and file, 3d artillery—to proceed in the next steamer (21st October) to reinforce Major Rains. This force reached its destination and joined in time to take an active part in the campaign.

Action of the governor of Oregon.—Major Rains' call of the 9th October for volunteers was answered on the 16th. Although within a very few hours' reach of each other, eight days elapsed before the governor answered; and then he says to Major Rains, developments after the date of his requisition for four companies of Oregon volunteers to be mustered into the service of the United States had determined him (the governor) "to call into the field a regiment of mounted volunteers, under the command of J. W. Nesmith, brigadier general of Oregon militia. It is wholly impracticable to induce the citizens of Oregon to enrol for service in the suppression of any Indian hostilities under the organization prescribed by the rules and regulations of the United States army. I am therefore constrained to preserve a distinct military organization, under the authority of the territorial government, of the force in the field in pursuance of my proclamation."

The proclamation referred to calls for eight companies, and assigns as a reason that "the chief in command of the military force of the United States in this district having made a requisition upon the executive of Oregon for a volunteer force to aid in suppressing the attacks of hostile Indians." In assigning this reason the governor leaves one to infer that the number of companies called out in his proclamation is in accordance with the call of Major Rains; whilst, in fact, Major R. only called for half the number the generous executive organizes into an independent northern Oregon volunteer army.

The volunteers from Washington, and their acting governor, were less fastidious. Two companies of these promptly came forward at the call of their executive, and enrolled themselves in the United States service under the banner of Major Rains. In reference to their services General Wool says: "These truly patriotic officers, (Captain Newell and Captain Strong,) with their companies, have rendered important services in restraining the Klikatats from joining in the war with the Yakamas."

Major Rains left Fort Dalles on the 30th October, with about 350 regulars, for a campaign into the Yakama country, with twenty days' provisions. On the 4th November, when about twenty-five miles from the Dalles, (map 19,) he broke up some large caches of Indian provisions, taking away about ten mule loads and destroying twenty more, having captured a spy who revealed these caches. Acting Governor Mason visited him at Camp Yakama, opposite Fort Dalles, and conferred on him the rank of brigadier general of Washington Territory, and returned to his capital.

Simultaneously with the movement of these regulars, six companies of the independent northern army of Oregon volunteers, under Colonel Nesmith, moved into the Yakama country; and a battalion of this army, under Major Chin, filed off from Fort Dalles, taking the direction of Fort Walla-Walla, (map 20.)

On the return of Lieutenant Slaughter's little force to his position on White river, after the defeat of Major Haller, Captain Maloney, 4th infantry, took command, having increased the force in the field of the Puget's Sound district so as to number about 100 regulars, and one company of mounted Washington volunteers, under Captain Hayes, and started to cross the Cascade range, through the Nachess Pass, for the purpose of forming a junction with Major Rains, who, it was expected, would have simultaneously left Fort Dalles. As some delay necessarily occurred in the time of the starting of the latter, Captain Maloney was advised, and accordingly returned to White river 2d November. This proved a fortunate movement for the scattered population of the Puget's Sound district. After the departure of the regulars from this district for the Yakama country, the Indians on the west slope of the Cascade range, being in free communication with the victorious Yakamas on the east, through the Klikatat, Cowlitz, and Yakama (Snoqualme) Passes, had risen in arms—stimulated, no doubt, by the success of their brother Yakamas in their fight with Major Haller—and compelled a detachment of citizen rangers to resort to a house for defence. Captain Maloney sent a party with an express to Fort Steilacoom, which was attacked, and some of the persons killed by the Indians within one day's journey of the fort.

On the 3d a party of 50 regulars and 50 volunteers, under Lieutenant Slaughter, 4th infantry, detached for the purpose, attacked a large body, numbering, it was said, 150 or 200, and killed 30 Indians. On the 3d November, General Wool reports to the headquarters of the army as follows: "In addition to Captain Ord's company, which went by the last steamer, I have ordered to the scene of hostilities, in Washington, Captain Keyes' company at the Presidio, also a company from Fort Humboldt, and Captain Fitzgerald's company 1st dragoons, at Fort Lane, Oregon, to push on as fast as possible for Fort Dalles. Ample stores and ammunition have been forwarded, and I shall leave in the steamer of the 6th instant for the scene of war, where I will be able to explain more clearly the position of affairs. It will not be safe to move any more of the troops from their present positions, but I shall endeavor to avoid the necessity of recognizing volunteers in the United States service. We require more troops in this department, at least one regiment." On the 3d December the 9th regiment of infantry was ordered to reinforce the department of the Pacific.

General Wool started with his staff as soon as possible, after receiving (19th October) Major Rains' report, and having made all necessary arrangements with regard to forwarding supplies, &c., in the steamer California, taking Captain Keyes' company along, which left San Francisco 6th November, 1855, having on board—

Major General Wool, commanding department Pacific.

Major Townsend, assistant adjutant general.

Major Cross, chief quartermaster.

Major Lee, chief commissary.

Captain Cram, chief topographical engineer.

Lieutenant Bonnycastle, aid.

Lieutenant Arnold, aid.

Captain Keyes, 3d artillery.

Lieutenant McKeever, 3d artillery.

Brevet Major Reynolds, 3d artillery, (intending to land at Fort Orford, to take command of his company at that post.)

Mr. Ferguson and Mr. R. Lee, clerks to Major Cross and Major Lee.

It was the intention of the general to have the boat stop in at Fort Humboldt and take one company, and with two companies proceed as fast as possible to Fort Vancouver, the military centre of operations then going on in the Puget's Sound and Yakama districts.

On the evening of leaving San Francisco a storm commenced, the first one of the rainy season. This was a severe storm for the Pacific coast. It was impossible to land at Humboldt, or even to enter the bay. After beating off and on 24 to 36 hours, and the storm increasing, it was decided to proceed without the company of the 4th infantry. The next day it was found equally impossible to land at Fort Orford, owing to the same cause, and Major Reynolds was obliged to continue on board.

The steamer was then put towards the Columbia river, and nothing disastrous occurred until we reached the offing at the mouth of that river; the storm continuing with unabated fury, it was found impossible, without extreme risk, to cross the bar. Accordingly the boat was kept steaming off and on, all anxiously waiting for a favorable condition to allow an attempt to be made by the pilot to put her across the bar. While in this state of things one of the boilers burst and the boat took fire.

The scene was awful in the extreme. There we were in the very midst of the tremendous breakers of the mouth of the Columbia, that can only be appreciated by being seen, in a raging storm, with a boat in flames. The elements were all against us. The cool, collected conduct of Captain Dall, commander of the boat, and the cheerful obedience of his officers and crew, saved us, under Providence, from wreck and from fire. He ordered the pilot to put the boat directly for crossing the bar, and all steam to be crowded that could be generated in the other boiler, himself taking the helm from the pilot after the latter had announced to Dall that the boat and all on board must be lost. For one half hour in that awful state of suspense, Dall calmly, with a cheerful smile on his countenance, issued his orders for extinguishing the fire, directed his officers how to act, and himself the while steered the boat.

Captain Keyes' company of soldiers and their officers were very instrumental in extinguishing the fire. There was a large quantity of gunpowder on board; that nearest the part of the boat in flames was thrown overboard, lest the fire should reach it and blow us up.

During the struggle between the power of the engine and of the opposing waves and breakers, a tremendous reacting wave from the sea struck the boat in her stern; this, with the force of the steam, carried us over the bar into comparatively safe water; now redoubled energy was applied to extinguish the flames, and in a few minutes more it was announced "the fire is under."

For one hour and more all reasonable men on board expected we must be burnt to death, blown up by an explosion of gunpowder, or wrecked among the breakers. All three causes threatening simultaneously to destroy all on board. Besides the military, there were many passengers; all those intending to land at several places having been brought by, from the impossibility of entering the ports. By night, however, the steamer had gained a position inside of the bar, where anchor was cast, her disabled condition not allowing her to stem the tide now against us, and we retired to rest as we thought in sufficient safety to allow us to hope seeing the light of another day. But during the night the wind, blowing strong down the river, caused our anchor to drag, and the current swept us back within half a boat's length of the dreadful breakers, into which if we had gone nothing within the power of man could have saved us; but before actually reaching the jaws of this danger, again the courage and decision of Captain Dall were brought into requisition. He ordered hogsheads of bacon, which were on board, to be broached; and this fatty substance used for fuel raised steam so quickly that headway was given to the boat, and we escaped the devouring breakers and steamed 10 miles up the river to Astoria. Here we remained 24 hours for the engineers to patch the boiler, then started for Fort Vancouver; but, as bad luck seemed yet determined to attend the California, she got aground, and we were 24 hours getting off; after that we reached Fort Vancouver on the 17th November, having been 12 days making the run from San Francisco; a run, under ordinarily favorable circumstances, that would have been accomplished i five or six days.

Immediately on the arrival of the general, he reports: "Finding a reinforcement more necessary at Steilacoom than in any other section, I have ordered Captain Keyes there with his company. Finding it impossible to cross the bar at Humboldt, I did not bring with me a company from that place; I shall order it to Crescent City, to guard and escort the supplies to Forts Lane and Jones."

It is to be observed that the commanding general of the department of the Pacific at this time had much on hand demanding his attention. There were four fields in which active operations were going on, viz: the Rogue River country, of which the operations have been described in chapter VI; the Puget's Sound district, in which Captain Keyes had now to take the immediate charge: the Yakama district, in which Major Rains was operating with the regulars, and Colonel Nesmith with the volunteers; and the country from Fort Dalles, towards the Walla-Walla valley, in which another body of the independent northern Oregon volunteer army were acting under Major Chin. To these may be added a fifth field, in which it was expected hostilities would be immediately commenced, the southeast part of the State of California. Indeed, the difficulties there threatened to be of such a nature that the act of leaving his headquarters for the Columbia river country, in the minds of some, was of questionable propriety in a strictly military point of view, irrespective of personal considerations of soldierly zeal.

The general commanding the department, however, was now at a point where he was enabled better to judge for himself of the wants of the service, and of the plans to be pursued in this portion of his command, than if he had remained at Benicia.

In our chronicle of events up to 30th October, we left Rains and Nesmith penetrating the Yakama country, the former with 350 regulars and two companies of Washington volunteers, who mustered into service under his command, and the latter with six companies of the northern Oregon army, who would not muster into the United States service, and for this reason the former had no authority over the latter; the Oregon volunteers, however, would go where went the regulars, and their presence greatly embarrassed the campaign; one of the exploits of this volunteer force consisted in burning the Catholic mission on the A-tah-nam, (map 19.)

So large a force as the regulars and volunteers in the Yakama field at the same time was calculated to frighten the Indians, and the consequence was, no battle could be had; some skirmishes occurred, amounting to nothing decisive.

In reporting upon this campaign General Wool says: "I regret the destruction of this mission by the volunteers who followed under the command of Colonel Nesmith, and ordered into the field at an enormous expense by Governor Curry, where they were not required, without my sanction or that of Major Rains."

Major Rains in his march, 300 miles, going and returning, drove the Indians beyond his reach, over mountains covered with snow; they fled to the northern part of their country, but did not in any considerable numbers cross the Columbia into the Nez Percé or Spokane country. This was in reality a winter campaign for the regulars; the snow had fallen to a considerable depth, and the troops were severely frozen in the feet; in several places the snow was waded through five feet deep, the animals were worn out, the men had become reduced in clothing, particularly in shoes and stockings; and those troops were destitute of all the necessary means to make another winter campaign.

The volunteers under Colonel Nesmith returned to Fort Dalles, from the Yakama country, 19th November.

General Wool reports, "Major Rains could follow the Indians no further on account of snow, then rapidly falling, being several feet deep; the intervening mountains covered with snow from two to three feet deep. He left the greater part of his regulars about 25 miles from Fort Dalles on the 20th to build a block-house, and arrived himself at Fort Vancouver on the 24th November."

After receiving the report of Major Rains, the general directed that the regulars of the Yakama campaign should be assembled at Fort Dalles for subsequent operations.

Three officers of his staff, Major Cross, Major Townsend, and Captain Cram, were directed to proceed to Fort Dalles, and Major Lee, with Captain Keyes, to Fort Steilacoom, each with instructions to inspect in reference to his appropriate department, and report upon the condition of the troops, the means of making another expedition that season, and the nature of the country into which the expedition should penetrate, the best to accomplish objects in a manner to be productive of some practical benefit.

It was apparent that little had been done, except to break down the command, in Major Rains' expedition, in company with volunteers. It was also apparent to the general, as well as to every intelligent army officer who had seen the operations of this independent organization of volunteers, that as long as they were permitted to remain in the field, very little, if anything, could be accomplished towards an effectual closing of troubles in that quarter.

General Wool also reports: "Unknown to Major Rains or myself, it would seem that the governor of Oregon, when he authorized or ordered Colonel Nesmith to follow Major Rains in his expedition to the Yakama country, he ordered four companies in the direction of Walla-Walla. These companies, under Major Chin, left Fort Dalles November 10, marched to the Umatilla, where they built a blockhouse and there waited reinforcements. After the return of Colonel Nesmith from the Yakama field, he ordered several companies (170 men) to reinforce Major Chin. During this period of more than two weeks, although the volunteers reported more than 1,000 Indians at or near Fort Walla-Walla, they were not attacked or molested by the Indians."

The superintendent of Indian affairs of Oregon writes to General Wool, November 21, 1855, as follows:

"The strong desire of a portion of our citizens to involve the tribes (Walla-Wallas, Cayuses, and Umatillas) with those (the Yakamas and Klikatats) now unfortunately engaged in hostilities against us, leads them to circulate exaggerated reports of the intentions and actions, well calculated to exasperate our people to acts of violence, with a view of provoking retaliation, which may afford an excuse for making war upon them. My confidence in the chief, Pee-pee-mox-mox, head chief of the Walla-Wallas, is such that I am unwilling to believe that he will engage in hostilities against us, unless driven and provoked to do so by overt acts of aggression on the part of our citizens. I am also satisfied that the Cayuses as a tribe are desirous of maintaining peace, and that there must be, on the part of the whites, a departure from the principles of justice, and a violation of the rights secured to this tribe by the treaty, before they will become a hostile party in this war. This is also true of the Nez Percés. Their uniform good conduct and friendship for our citizens render all intention on their part to make war on us as quite improbable. The reported combination of all those tribes with intent to wage a war of extermination against the whites is, I apprehend, but a phantom conjured up in the brains of alarmists, unsupported by one substantial reason."

On the same date (November 21) as the foregoing, Colonel Nesmith, of the independent northern Oregon volunteer army, made a requisition on the commanding general of the department of the Pacific, as follows:

"It is reported that Pee-pee-mox-mox, with his 1,000 warriors, had taken a strong position. To dislodge him it is desirable to have the service of artillery. I have therefore to request you will furnish me with two or three howitzers, or other equivalent artillery, with officers and men requisite to manage the same, for that purpose."

To which the general replied, November 24, "I have not the power to give you the assistance you ask for."

The careful reader will here observe that the responsible officer, viz: the superintendent of Indian affairs, presents a very different view of the case to the responsible general commanding the department from that presented at identically the same time by the irresponsible officer of the volunteers, in relation to the very grave question of carrying the sword into the Umatilla country. The responsible officer makes no requisition upon General Wool, while the commander of the governor's independent northern army seeks to induce the general to embark the regulars in the enterprise.

Now, what was the real condition of the settlers in the Walla-Walla and Umatilla valleys at this time? A few whites had been permitted to go there on sufferance by the Indian agent, for, be it observed, none of that country as yet had had the Indian title extinguished; but in granting this permission to the whites to enter it, it was well understood by them that they were to depart at any time at the bidding of the agent.

All the whites had left those regions and come into places of safety nearly a month before Chin's command started thither from Fort Dalles, and this, too, on warning of Indian Agent Olney, immediately after learning of Haller's defeat. The half-breeds, however, of whom there were a few families, having nothing to fear, remained. There were two houses belonging to the whites that had been thus deserted, also the Hudson Bay Company store at the mouth of the Walla-Walla. There is proof to show that it was not Pee-pee-mox-mox, but Yellow Serpent, who pillaged the store, and that it was a Nez Percé, at the instigation of the Yakamas, who burnt the houses.

It was well known to General Wool that the report of Chin being threatened with 1,000 warriors was an exaggerated fabrication, for the warriors of the Walla-Wallas, the Umatillas, and Cayuses, all together could not exceed 300.

The governor of Oregon had called out volunteers to send to the Walla-Walla country before the pillaging of the fort and the burning of the deserted houses, and that the Indians there had nothing favorable to hope at the hands of these volunteers was the common belief in all that country.

The houses had been plundered and burnt and the stock driven off before Chin's command left Fort Dalles, but not until after the war had been carried into the Yakama country by Major Haller, contrary to the expectations of his commanding officer who sent him, and not until after Chin had received orders to march through the Umatilla and Walla-Walla countries. His orders were (as he informed the writer) to march to the Walla-Walla, thence to the Snake river, to the assistance of Governor Stevens; and if he met Indians hostile to treat them as such, but to treat friendly Indians with favor.

When a governor, who is not the superintendent of Indian affairs in his Territory, sends an armed force of volunteers into a fertile valley in which the Indians are known to have fine, fat beeves and excellent horses in herds of great abundance, it will be readily inferred that with such very general orders, so loosely given as were those to Major Chin, it would be a very easy matter, upon the smallest pretext, to draw or provoke the Indians into a fight, and afterwards justify the act, particularly as in such cases there is only one side whose story is seldom, if ever, told to the world. Now, I do not mean to say that these volunteers were sent into the valley of the Walla-Walla for the purpose of plundering those Indians of their beeves and horses, but it is fair to conclude that they never would have gone with the almost certain prospect of being obliged to winter there, but from the fact, well known among them, that there would be plenty found there to subsist themselves during the winter, to refit themselves with horses, and to make themselves comfortable and warm.

If the governor's independent northern Oregon volunteer army were really desirous of making another winter campaign against Indians known to be hostile, they had only to follow the Yakamas into their winter retreats, and then they would have received some credit for disinterestedness.

Major Chin having been reinforced, as stated, Lieutenant Colonel Kelly took command, and started from the Umatilla, where they had named their block-house Fort Henrietta, on the night of the 2d December, and encamped on the Walla-Walla, three miles above its mouth, and scouting parties were sent out.

Here is a point for inquiry, Was it the Indians or volunteers who fired the first shot? Lieutenant Colonel Kelly has never answered this ; but Indian Agent Olney, who was all the while with this expedition, reports "that soon after they arrived here a party of Indians were seen on the hills, when a detachment of volunteers commenced a fire upon them."

On the 5th, Lieutenant Colonel Kelly divided his force, sending Major Chin with 125 men to escort his baggage and pack-trains to the mouth of the Touchet, (map 20,) and himself started with the remainder for a point fifteen miles above, on the same stream, where Pee-pee-mox-mox, chief of the Walla-Wallas, and his warriors were encamped. Lieutenant Colonel Kelly himself says : "When within three miles of the hostile village, that chieftain, with about seventy or eighty armed warriors, made his appearance, approaching towards us. An order was at once given to attack them; but as we moved rapidly up I observed six or seven Indians, a short distance in advance of their main body, bearing a white flag. Halting my command, I went where they were with Agent Olney, an interpreter, and three or four others. One of these Indians was the chief, Pee-pee-mox-mox, who asked why we had come armed into his country, and was told we came to chastise him and his people for the wrongs they had done to the whites. He said he desired peace; that he did not wish to fight, and that he had done us no wrong. I recapitulated the wrongs, the pillaging and destruction of Fort Walla-Walla, and appropriating the goods, the burning of the houses, and the driving off the cattle. At first he denied having done these, but afterwards said they were done by his young men, and that he could not restrain them. He said he would make his people restore the goods taken by them so far as they could be restored, and pay for the balance. I stated to him that this would not be sufficient; that, in addition, he should make his people surrender their arms and ammunition, give us cattle for beef, and horses to remount my command. To these terms he consented, and said he would come on the morrow and comply with them. I told him that we came to wage war against him, and that he could not go without exposing his villages to immediate attack; I told him he might go away under his flag of truce, but that if he did so we would without delay commence an attack on his villages; that if he and his six followers would consent to remain and fulfil the terms his tribe would not be molested."

Lieutenant Colonel Kelly held the chief and his companions prisoners, and, while holding their chief as prisoner, tried to induce the people to comply with his demands; but finding his negotiations to compel them to despoil themselves of arms, ammunition, beeves, and horses, and seeing no hope of coming to terms, he marched down to the mouth of the Touchet, taking his prisoners along, and tied them on the night of the 6th, one having attempted, but unsuccessfully, to escape. It is also in the evidence of two captains of these volunteers, that "on the morning of the 7th a party of Indians appeared on the hills in front of our camp. Here Lieutenant Colonel Kelly sent another messenger asking them to come in and give up their arms. They again refused, but demanded of us their chief, and ordered us to pass no further up the river, or they would fight us."

Disregarding this warning, the volunteers started about 8 o'clock the same morning to march up the Walla-Walla river, and had gone about three-fourths of a mile "when the Indians fired at two men who were driving up some loose beef cattle." It is not reported whether these beeves belonged of right to the volunteers or the Indians; but the report goes on to say "the fire was returned and a general fight ensued."

Lieutenant Colonel Kelly accuses the Indians with firing first this morning, but Mr. Olney reports: "I am forced to believe the firing was first commenced by the volunteers, as it was evident the Indians did not meditate an attack, for they were at the same time preparing the morning meal; in several places the volunteers dismounted and partook of the roast beef found at the fires where the Indians were encamped."

The Indians were driven ten miles up the Walla-Walla, to La Rogue's house, (now called Fort Bennet,) when they were reinforced and made a stand. The prisoners, Pee-pee-mox-mox and his companions, were brought up by the guard. Kelly says: "On the sergeant of the guard saying to me they were greatly excited while the battle was raging, and that he feared they would escape, I told him to tie them all; and if they resisted or attempted to escape, to kill them.''

After giving this order, the commanding officer says he ''rode on, and when about 200 yards distant, heard the report of fire-arms at the place where the prisoners were, and was shortly informed that when my order to tie them was about being carried into effect, they resisted, one having drawn a concealed knife from his coat sleeve, with which he wounded Sergeant Miller in the arm. Pee-pee-mox-mox attempted to wrest a gun from the hands of one of our men, when he was knocked down with the butt of a rifle, and put to death, as were also all the other prisoners, except a Nez Percé youth, who made no resistance at being tied.''

After the foregoing evidence from his own mouth, it may be pertinent to ask if Lieutenant Colonel Kelly will again accuse, to the governor of Oregon, ''an officer of the United States army at Fort Vancover'' of putting in circulation untrue reports concerning the capture and death of the late chief of the Walla-Wallas?

''After coming to a stand at La Rogue's, the Indians fought the volunteers desperately until dark on the 7th; on the 8th the battle was renewed, and the fight continued until night, when both parties again withdrew; on the 9th the Indians again made their appearance, when they were attacked by our party. This day's fighting was not so hard as the former. Early on the morning of the 10th the Indians had got possession of our trenches; a party was sent out to attack them; a hot fire was kept up five or six hours, when the Indians were routed, and all were driven far above their camping ground, left the field, and were seen no more. On the field, our loss was 16 wounded and 6 killed. The loss of the enemy was not definitely ascertained.''

The Indians during this fight were removing their effects across the Snake river, and after the battle the warriors who had so bravely covered the retreat also crossed it. The northern army of Oregon volunteers went into winter quarters, and there rested upon their laurels, regaling themselves upon the beeves of the luxuriant valley of the Walla-Walla.

The Cayuse chief, Howlish Wampum, the very friend and identical man whom Lieutenant Colonel Kelly brought forward to sustain his accusation against Pee-pee-mox-mox, says: ''We had thousands of horses and cattle; the hills and valleys were covered with them; where are they now? Not an animal is to be seen over this wide expanse. Between the hostile Indians and the (volunteers) we are stripped of everything.''

In regard to the operations in the Puget's Sound district.—On the 4th October the United States sloop-of-war ''Decatur,'' Commander J. S. Sterrett, anchored off the little town of Seattle.

On November 22 the Decatur was at Steilacoom.

On November 24 Captain Keyes, with his company, arrived at Fort Steilacoom, having been despatched by General Wool, as before stated, from Fort Vancouver.

On the 25th, Lieutenant Slaughter's camp, on the Puyallup, 21 miles

from the fort, was surrounded, his sentinels fired on, and in the night
32 animals were stolen.

On the receipt of this, Captain Keyes took the field, leaving Captain Maloney, with 100 men, in command of the fort. The hostile Indians in this district were principally located in a densely wooded country admirably adapted to ambuscade, and full of trails crossing in every direction. Pack animals had to be used for transportation. The Captain says, "as our pack animals are small in number, and nearly broken down by hard work, and as there is a lack of feed in the places where the troops have to operate, we may be reduced shortly to the necessity of acting entirely on the defensive, and must wait for summer and a larger force before we can subdue the Indians."

On December 1 the Decatur again anchored at Seattle, where her commander received a request from the citizens for protection against the northern Indians.

Commander Sterrett reports, December 5: "After several interviews with these Indians, I have the satisfaction to state that they have consented to depart, and have promised not to return during the Indian troubles."

For the opportune arrival of the Decatur in these waters, and the timely assistance rendered by her to the citizens, the Hon. Secretary of War tendered his acknowledgments to Commander Sterrett.

On the evening of 5th December, while encamped near the junction of Green and White rivers, (map 16,) Lieutenant Slaughter was picked off by Indians, who crawled up near his camp, guided by the light of a fire he had imprudently allowed to be kindled. In reporting his death, also that of two corporals, and the wounding of six privates on that occasion, the commanding general says: " Lieutenant Slaughter was a gallant and enterprising officer, and had rendered important services in the defence of the inhabitants of the Puget's Sound district."

Captain (Brevet Major) Fitzgerald's company 1st dragoons arrived at Fort Vancouver about the 1st December, having made the march from Fort Lane, 278 miles, with their wagon train, in 21 days, under the most unfavorable condition of the roads.

On the 13th December the commanding general reports: "The Indians will not engage in a field fight with any considerable number of regulars. Their mode is one of ambush and surprise. Their country, both in Oregon and Washington, except near Puget's Sound, being mountainous, is well calculated for this mode of warfare. Under these circumstances it would be exceedingly difficult, with my present limited force, however well prepared, which is not the case, to either conquer or bring these Indians to terms in this region by chasing them—all being well mounted—through the mountains; and certainly not at the present moment, the mountains being generally covered with snow several feet deep. They can only be conquered or brought to terms by occupying their country in such positions as to command their fisheries and the valleys where their cattle and horses are grazed. This I propose to do; and I am now, with my staff, actually preparing an expedition for this purpose.

This, however, after a critical inspection of troops, supplies, and means, I find cannot be accomplished as soon as I could wish, owing to the want of troops, means of transportation and clothing for the 4th infantry. The several expeditions—viz: to Fort Boisé, returned the last of September; the recent one of Major Haller to the Yakama country; and the more recent one of Major Rains into the same country—have reduced the greater part of the horses and mules of the command, including those of Major Fitzgerald's company, just arrived from Fort Lane, to a condition which renders them for the time being unfit for service. As soon as the animals are fit for service my present force will be ready to take the field; and if I should receive, in the meantime, an additional force of one regiment, which would supersede the necessity of employing so expensive a force as volunteers, I have no doubt I will be able in a short time to conquer the Indians in Oregon and Washington, or compel them to sue for peace or abandon their country. I have in no instance received or authorized the raising of volunteers. I have adhered to this rule because I applied to the Secretary of War for the authority, which was not granted.

"When this war was sprung upon us the regular force under my command, in order to give equal protection to the inhabitants, was dispersed in small commands from the northern to the southern extremity of the department, extending over more than 1,600 miles; but not a sufficient force at any one point to overcome a combined attack of several tribes of Indians. If the Indians in the southeast portion of the department should make war on the people in that section, I could send no relief besides the troops at Fort Yuma and San Diego, which would not exceed 250 rank and file, except by withdrawing troops from the Yakama field, the Puget's Sound field, or the Rogue river field. This could not be done at the present time without endangering the settlements in Washington, Oregon, and northern California.

"In conclusion, it is justly due to make known that the sudden, unexpected, and arduous duties which the officers of the line, as well as of the staff, have been called on to discharge, were zealously, promptly, and efficiently executed. All deserve high commendation."

On the 18th December the United States Coast Survey steamer Active, Commander Alden, having volunteered for the service of the war, appeared in the Puget's Sound waters. At this time operations in this district had for the most part ceased for the winter, owing to the small force which could be brought into the field and the condition of the country, which, from incessant rains, had become almost impassable. The regulars and volunteers had been drawn in around the towns to act on the defensive, making occasional demonstrations against the Indians.

On the 25th December the general reports: "Since my communication of the 13th instant winter has fairly set in, the ground is covered with snow, and the Columbia river is frozen over as low down as the mouth of the Willamette, six miles below this place, [Fort Vancouver.] This cuts off all communication with Fort Dalles and the whole country above until the river is clear of ice. Owing to the high water in the streams it has been impracticable to send reinforcements by land to Fort Steilacoom. I intended to have sent Captain Ord's company, 3d artillery, but have failed in my efforts to procure transportation until the ice breaks up. I can send no reinforcement to Captain Keyes."

With the two vessels-of-war in the Puget's Sound waters, and the regulars and the volunteers in that district, the general was satisfied the inhabitants could be defended until he would be able to send a reinforcement; but he did not expect the troops would be able to take the offensive until Captain Keyes could be reinforced.

The general says: "In my communication to the headquarters of the army, 13th December, I mentioned that I was actively engaged in preparing an expedition for the Indian country. I soon found it would be impracticable to execute my intentions as soon as I desired. I could neither obtain in this country the means of transportation nor forage without paying enormously for them, which the state of the war in this region did not call for. This state of things has been caused by the extraordinary course pursued by the governor of Oregon, who is making war against the Indians on his own account, and without the slightest reference to myself, not having received any communication whatever from him on the subject. The quantity of supplies required for his volunteers and the enormous prices paid in scrip by his agents have rendered it necessary for me to resort to Benicia for horses and mules, and to San Francisco for forage."

The governor of Oregon says: "On my return from southern Oregon I learned from those representing me, who had made General Wool an official visit in my absence, of the inauguration of a plan utterly at variance with my own, which obviated the necessity of a personal interview. The wisdom of my plans it remains only, in part, for time to vindicate."

The governor was very much in error in supposing any official communication, by any one claiming to represent him, was made to General Wool, or to any officer of his staff.

It is true, that as soon as the war commenced, then, indeed, were the general and his troops vociferously called for in Washington and Oregon, but not by the governor of the latter Territory. Their papers, teemed with articles, as if to convince the readers that the only duty of this veteran soldier, whose head had become hoar in the service of his country, now consisted in standing, in person, at every man's door, in both Territories, with his drawn sword to defend its inmates from the ruthless savage ! And when the general promptly repaired with the vigor of youth to the very military centre of the scene, and dared to issue his commands and express his opinions, as it well became an officer clothed with responsible trusts of honor and authority, and ready to exert that authority without the aid of the army of volunteers whom the governor of Oregon had called out and thrust into the field, then it was that these papers in Oregon were lavish with abuse of the general and the regular army; and the legislature of that Territory, as an everlasting monument to its members, passed a memorial requesting the President to recall General Wool from the command; and this, too, while he was personally superintending, and in the very act of devising those judicious means which will be shown in the sequel did give defence to the frontier settlements and terminated hostilities.

The governor of Oregon forwarded this memorial to the President; but finding that no action was taken upon it, the governor afterwards sent his approval of the memorial, and requested again the recall of the general, but with as little effect as before. I venture to say a more unjust document never emanated from a legislative body. I will not pollute this paper with its contents, except to quote one passage, which runs, "we [the memorialists] are compelled to say that General Wool has hitherto remained inactive, and has refused to send the United States troops to the relief of the volunteers, or to supply them with arms and ammunition in time of need."

The first point of this accusation is totally refuted by what I have already detailed in relation to the action of General Wool and the troops under his command.

The second point gives us the key to the policy of the governor's plan; it leaves one to infer that it consisted in using the regulars as "hewers of wood and drawers of water;" in short, to play second to the volunteers who would not serve under United States officers, but would have these and the soldiers serve under the volunteers; in other words, for carrying on the war, the plan of the governor of a Territory contemplated making the President's military commander of a department and his troops subservient to territorial executive influence.

In relation to the third point, "refusing to supply the volunteers with arms and ammunition," the answer is, that the volunteers had been supplied with arms and ammunition from the United States depot at Fort Vancouver by the storekeeper, who, by so doing, acted contrary to law made and provided; and it was to this law that the general had reference when he declined to send artillery to Colonel Nesmith.

In this remarkable legislative memorial we have the best possible evidence to show that the commanding general's measures for restoring peace and suppressing hostilities were very much in the way of what has been alleged of the designs which animated the zeal of some of the officers and of the advocates of the governor's northern volunteer army, whose origin, organization, and acts, in some measure, have been explained.

The country and the War Department have reason to congratulate themselves on having one in command of the department capable and bold enough, while performing his military duties, to prevent them from being perverted at so critical a juncture of affairs in that quarter to other than the legitimate objects of the honor and trust confided in him.

The President did not see fit to recall his general, and leave the military operations of the United States army in the hands of the executive of Oregon; and General Wool continued to pursue the even tenor of his way, quite undisturbed by the petulancy of the Oregon legislature, of the members of whom it may be said truly that in this memorial they exhibit themselves as an apt illustration of the fact that the people of a colony, after all, are but children of the home government.

In his report of the 3d December, 1855, the Hon. Secretary of War, in alluding to these volunteers, says: "And it is hoped that their continuance in the military service, to the great interruption of their ordinary pursuits, will be limited to the shortest possible duration by the arrival of reinforcements, which have been ordered to the regular troops of that department."

"In regard to what volunteer reinforcements to the regular troops may be necessary, this is a matter which must be necessarily left to the military commander in the department of the Pacific, who has repaired to the theatre of hostilities."

After the foregoing gentle hints to his excellency of Oregon, it might have been supposed his northern army of volunteers would have been disbanded; not so, however. The governor still kept them in their winter quarters in the Walla-Walla valley, and, instead of limiting their time to the "shortest possible," found it more consistent with his own plan to extend their services to the longest possible duration.

On the 21st December T. B. Cornelius was made colonel of the volunteers, after which, in February, his command was increased by four companies, making it now one regiment, numbering about 550 persons.

The governor of Oregon took up his headquarters at Fort Dalles on the 15th February, whence he issued his commands. Whether he consulted on the present occasion that "vigilant officer of the efficient 4th infantry," by whose information the governor professes to have been influenced on a former occasion, I will not pretend to say. It seems to have been here that he planned a spring campaign for his volunteers, and directed Colonel Cornelius to follow it. The sapient governor presumed to know that the "main body of the Indians were between the Snake and Pelouse rivers, on the south side of the Columbia, and it was there that they might be drawn into a pitched battle," (map 21.)

The ambition of Colonel Cornelius was stimulated by being urged to open the campaign and conquer the Indians before the United States troops could take the field, which the governor says, "I anticipate will be about the middle of April, and confidently expect, before that time, the volunteers will have achieved the purpose for which they were called out."

His excellency refers to his admirable organization of the staff, who would furnish the colonel with ample supplies, &c.

The new colonel, obedient to the governor's orders, begins to shell his volunteers out of their comfortable winter quarters as early as the 9th of March, determined to anticipate the regulars. I have carefully studied the colonel's report of this campaign, and find that from the 9th of March to the 2d of April they went groping along the lower parts of the Snake, Pelouse, and Yakama rivers, occasionally killing a straggling Indian, but without finding the "main body of Indians" which the governor had said were there. Colonel Cornelius reports that there were no "manifestations that the country had been occupied during the past winter by any large body of Indians."

During this campaign the volunteers were reduced to the strait of living on horse flesh, the governor's boasted commissariat having failed to supply them, and, alas, discontent arose among the volunteers. Indeed, they were so much reduced in means of living and in horses, that on the 30th of March the colonel ordered part of his command to Fort Dalles, *via* the south side of the Columbia, and himself, with the other portion, proceeded through the Yakama country, *via* the north side, towards the fort, intending, as he said, to scour the Klikatat valley. And thus this campaign ended in perfect nullity; and all will agree with the governor in his assertion that "the wisdom of his plans it remains for time to vindicate."

On the 11th of January, 1856, the mail steamer brought to General Wool, then at Fort Vancouver, important despatches in reference to the threatened Indian hostilities (already referred to) in the southeast part of California, and the pleasing information of the arrival of the 9th regiment of infantry at San Frascisco to reinforce his department. Orders had been issued previously for the disposition of this regiment. The despatches were of such a nature as to make it necessary for him to return to Benicia to give his personal attention to the wants of the southern portion of his command, not only in California, but in southern Oregon likewise. Accordingly the general left Fort Vancouver the same night, (11th January,) and on his way passed the colonel's (Wright's) portion of the 9th infantry going up to take post temporarily at Fort Vancouver, and met the other portion, under Lieutenant Colonel Casey, which was to operate in Puget's Sound. A personal interview was had by the general, on the Pacific ocean, with the lieutenant colonel, to whom orders were given.

The last report from Captain Keyes had informed the general that, "in the region of Puget's Sound, there were not to exceed 200 warriors in arms against the whites."

The general reports, headquarters Benicia, January 19, 1856:

"You will perceive that I have returned, after being ice-bound three weeks. The severity of the season has cut off all communication with Fort Dalles. Owing to the snow on the Cascade mountains there is no route during the winter to that post other than by the Columbia; and that, for several weeks past, has been frozen over as low down as St. Helen's; it is, however, now open to Fort Vancouver. The 9th infantry has passed on to Fort Vancouver and Puget's Sound; the colonel with eight companies to the former, and the lieutenant colonel with two companies to the latter. Captain Ord's company 3d artillery is ordered to return, to be sent, if necessary, to the Colorado, where an Indian war is threatened. I shall also order Captain Keyes' company to return from the Puget's Sound district, for the same destination, if it should become necessary.

"With the 9th and 4th infantry I have no doubt of being able, in a short time after we can take the field, to terminate the war in the north and in southern Oregon, unless the crusade of the governor of Oregon against Indians inhabiting Washington Territory should prevent. By sending his volunteers against the Walla-Wallas, who had not made open war against the whites, he has added several tribes to the ranks of the enemy."

It will be perceived that Colonel George Wright and Lieutenant Colonel Silas Casey, of the 9th infantry, were now in command, the former in the Columbia River district, and the latter in the Puget's Sound district.

On the return of Governor Stevens to his capital, Olympia, January 19, he says : "In obedience to my own convictions of duty, and in response to the sentiments of this entire community, I issued my proclamation calling for six companies of volunteers for the defence of the Sound, and three companies to operate east of the Cascades, &c.   *   * Since my arrival the town of Seattle has been attacked," &c.   *   *

Previously to Casey's taking the command, the Indians suddenly appeared in the woods immediately back of and fired upon that town. There were guarding it at the time one company of volunteers and the sloop-of-war Decatur. There were probably as many whites in the village as there were attacking Indians. It was reported that by the Decatur's guns 36 Indians were killed and 35 wounded, and that the hostiles numbered all the way from 300 up to 1,500. Subsequent investigations, however, showed that they only numbered 70 to 75, and that there was no proof of one being killed. The Indians had secreted themselves behind trees and logs before firing, and, as they were not charged, there they remained till the sport became stale, and then deliberately walked away.

At this time the inhabitants of Puget's Sound were in a straitened condition indeed; the whole country from Green river south to within five miles of Fort Steilacoom, had been conquered, and was occupied by hostile Indians.

Lieutenant Colonel Casey at once commenced his work, by opening a communication from the fort to Muckleshoot prairie, where he established a block-house.

On or about the 27th February the principal chief, Kanasket, of the hostiles was shot by a sentinel (Private Kehl, D company, 9th infantry,) while endeavoring, in the night, with four others, to steal into Lieutenant Colonel Casey's camp. He was the most savage of all the chiefs.

On the morning of 1st March a detachment under Lieutenant Kautz, at the crossing of White river, about two miles above Muckleshoot prairie, (map 16,) found himself cut off from camp by a body of Indians in his rear. The lieutenant determined to hold his position, and despatched a note to camp, to apprise the commanding officer, and put his men for safety behind drift wood. About 1 o'clock a party of Indians, from the other side of the river, fired into Kautz's party and wounded two of his men.   At 2 o'clock, Captain Keyes' command appeared on the left bank, and found Kautz's party, under cover of drift wood, engaged with the Indians on both banks.

Keyes drove the Indians who were on the left bank, then returned to a point above, crossed his command over the river by fording, and then charged the main body from their position behind logs and trees, on Kautz's side of the river, and completely routed them; then wheeling his company to the left, deployed as skirmishers, and charged on through the woods, sending orders to Kautz, as soon as they should arrive opposite his position, to leave his drift and join, which he did; and the two bodies of troops all moved forward rapidly, and drove the Indians from the point of woods they occupied below.   The Indians continued to retreat and the troops to pursue for two miles, till they reached the bluff which borders the river bottom, at the top of which they made a stand.

The bluff is 150 feet high, with a slope of about 45°, and free from underbrush, with but few trees.   As the troops advanced the Indians taunted and defied them to come on, with many vile epithets.   The troops rushed forward, routed, and completely dispersed the enemy. Here the action terminated at dark, after five hours' duration.

Keyes' loss was one killed, nine wounded, including Lieutenant Kautz.   The loss on the part of the Indians could not be ascertained. The number of Indians engaged was about 200, and the troops numbered 116, officers included.

This was an important action; it broke the spirits of the Indians; it was the opinion that all the hostile warriors, except their sentinels who were guarding trails, were present.   Captain Keyes, in his report, says : "We have now the good fortune of having completely routed the Indians; our next difficulty will be to find them."

On 5th March Captain Keyes was sent, with 120 men, to attack their main camp, which was found to be from Muckleshoot about six miles towards Porter's prairie, in the middle of a swamp, defended by a breastwork of logs with loop holes, but the Indians had fled the night before.

After their defeat by Keyes, the Indians in Puget's Sound district began to scatter in small parties, taking to their hiding places.

On the 21st February the general notified Lieutenant Colonel Casey of his intention to reinforce him with two companies.

We must now leave the Puget's Sound district for a while, and pass to the Columbia river operations.

On the 29th January, 1856, the general commanding the department directed Colonel Wright, 9th infantry, as follows:

"As soon as the season will permit, preparatory to operations in the Indian country east and north of the Cascade mountains, you will establish the headquarters of your regiment at Fort Dalles, where all the troops intended for said country will be concentrated.

"The points which I intend as the base of operations are the Selah fishery, on the Yakama river, (map 19,) and some point in the neighborhood of Fort Walla-Walla, (map 20.)   It is my intention to establish a permanent post in this region at the most eligible point for controlling the surrounding Indian tribes.

"Between Fort Dalles and Selah fishery an intermediate post with one company may be necessary to prevent the Yakamas from taking fish on the tributaries of the Yakama and Columbia. Herewith you will receive a memoir and sketches (17, 18, 19, 20, 21,) by Captain Cram, chief of the Topographical Engineers, of the country in which your command will be required to operate. I would recommend it to your attentive perusal. From this you will perceive it is 100 miles from Fort Dalles to Selah fishery, and 70 from the Fort to the At-ah-nam mission. This latter position may be important as the intermediate post between the Dalles and the fishery.

"From Fort Dalles to Fort Walla-Walla it is 142 miles, and from the latter place to Selah fishery it is 95 miles by the road to Fort Steilacoom. With boats to cross the Columbia, your forces at either point could be in a few days concentrated.

"Expeditions should be prepared at the earliest moment, that is, as soon as grass can be obtained for the animals for Walla-Walla and the Selah fishery. As the snow will not probably allow the expedition to the latter so early by three or four weeks, the one to the former will be undertaken as soon as the season will permit with four or five companies and three howitzers; it is desirable this expedition should be conducted with reference to selecting a proper position for a post, and to ascertain the feelings and dispositions of the several tribes in that section of country; I do not believe they will continue the war a great while. The occupation of the country between the Walla-Walla, Touchet, and Snake rivers, and the opposite side of the Columbia, (map 21,) will very soon bring those tribes to terms. The occupation at the proper time of the Yakama country, (map 17,) from the At-ah-nam mission, and that on the Yakama river above and below the Selah fishery, will compel the Yakamas, I think, to sue for peace or abandon their country.

"By the memoir of Captain Cram, herewith sent, you will perceive that obstacles on the routes to both the Fishery and Walla-Walla will require your attention. On fitting out your expeditions pioneer parties should be organized."

Such, in substance, were the instructions despatched to Colonel Wright, 20th January, for his guidance in the coming operations, which were to be commenced as soon as the Columbia should be open to Fort Dalles.

In the topographical memoir of Captain Cram particular mention had been made of the importance in military operations of the Cascades, 45 miles above Fort Vancouver, (map 18.) Major Rains had erected a block-house here and garrisoned it with one sergeant and ten men in the preceding autumn.

On the 6th February the general received a requisition from the superintendent of Indian affairs in Oregon for one company of regulars, to be stationed in the Cayuse Indian country, to protect the friendly Cayuses from the volunteers, accompanying the requisition with a representation from high authority as follows:

"January 15, the volunteers, without discipline, without order, and similar to the madmen of the revolution, menace us with death every day; they have already despoiled of their provisions the inhabitants of this country and the Indians who have so nobly followed the advice to remain faithful friends of the Americans.

"To-day these same volunteers are not yet satisfied with rapine and injustice, and wish to take away the small remnant of animals and provisions left. Every day they run off the horses of the friendly Indians," * * * &c.

The Cayuse reservation is on the Umatilla at the point marked "Agency," map 20.

On the 7th February the general directed Colonel Wright as follows: "At the earliest moment practicable, agreeably to previous instructions, you will send four companies to the Walla-Walla country. Should, you however, find, on the arrival of the troops in the Cayuse country, that a company is necessary to give protection to the Cayuse Indians from the volunteers, you will leave a company there with a howitzer and ammunition."

On the 6th of March the Indians on the north side of the Columbia, probably a foraging party of half-starved Klikatats, made a descent on Joselyn's farm, at the mouth of the White Salmon, about halfway between the Cascades and Fort Dalles, and robbed it of half the stock. On the receipt of this information Colonel Wright despatched Lieutenant Colonel Steptoe with two companies to that point, from Fort Vancouver, and followed on the 7th and 8th with all the troops destined for service in the Indian country above Fort Vancouver, and himself arrived at Fort Dalles 11th March.

The colonel posted a company temporarily at the head of the Cascades.

After giving the final instructions at Crescent City and Port Orford in relation to the operations described in chapter VI, in the Rogue river field of war, the general then proceeded to Columbia River district with the following members of his staff : Lieutenants Bonnycastle and Arnold, aids-de-camp; Captain Cram and Lieutenant Mendell, Topographical Engineers, and Assistant Surgeon Milhau, and arrived at Fort Vancouver on the night of 10th March.

Here, remaining long enough to receive reports and to give the necessary instructions to Colonel Wright, who was now on his way to Fort Dalles, the general decided to take two companies of the 9th infantry, (Fletcher's and Dent's,) which he placed under Major Garnett, of the same regiment, to reinforce the troops in the Puget's Sound district, and himself to proceed to Fort Steilacoom.

These were left to be under the immediate orders of Colonel Wright: one company 4th infantry at Fort Vancouver, and one company and part of another of dragoons; one company 3d artillery, eight companies infantry, at the Cascades, and above at Fort Dalles; when the general departed with Garnett's reinforcement.

On the 14th March this reinforcement arrived at Fort Steilacoom, and immediately entered the field. The general remained here to have an interview with Lieutenant Colonel Casey, inspect, and issue all needful orders for future operations, assigning Lieutenant Mendell as the topographical engineer in this field, and directing Captain Cram to make a reconnaissance along the waters of the Straits of Fuca, the Cape Flattery Indian coast, and return with despatches for the Rogue river field, thence to Benicia. Assistant Surgeon Milhau was sent down to Crescent City for duty in this field.

At this time, in the Puget's Sound field, Lieutenant Colonel Casey had six companies infantry and one company artillery of regulars under his command. In this field also were thirteen to seventeen companies, or skeletons of companies, of Washington volunteers, under the orders of the executive, stationed at certain points, but over these the United States army officer commanding the district had no control whatever, they not having been called out by him, but by the governor.

On the 15th March the commanding officer of the district called upon the executive of Washington for two companies of volunteers to be mustered into the United States service to serve on foot. The authority for the call was derived from the official report from the Hon. Secretary of War, wherein he says the number of volunteers to be called in to reinforce the regulars must be left to the judgment of the military commander of the department. Lieutenant Colonel Casey informed the governor that with his present force of regulars and the two companies of volunteers now called for, "I am of the opinion that I should have a sufficient force to protect this frontier without the aid of those volunteers now in this Territory."

To this requisition his excellency replied the next day: "I will state that the requisition will not be complied with. I do not consider it expedient to change the plan of campaign nor the organization of the troops so far as the volunteers are concerned."

On the 16th March the general, having given all necessary personal attention to the Puget's Sound district, left Fort Steilacoom to return to the scene of the Rogue river operations, and thence to Benicia, where he arrived about the 22d March.

With his regulars Lieutenant Colonel Casey took such active steps, after the departure of the general, that rapid progress was soon made in hunting out the hiding places of the parties into which the main body of hostiles was dispersed, however difficult of approach.

To Stuck prairie he sent an expedition, March 18, which attacked an Indian village and captured several Indians; sent another expedition with orders to attack a body supposed to be on Boisé creek; organized an expedition against the Indians on Dwamish lake, and requested Captain Swartwout, of the steamer Massachusetts, to co-operate with his boats, but he declined; after that these Indians came in.

The companies of Dent, Pickett, and Fletcher, under Major Garnett, made an expedition to Meridian prairie May 13, and afterwards scouted the country along Green and Cedar rivers. These scouts were very active in hunting for parties of Indians.

On the 19th May Lieutenant Colonel Casey reported the war west of the Cascade range of mountains at an end; and, on the 21st May, Major Garnett's command of two companies of the 9th were ordered to join Colonel Wright, who was operating in the Columbia River district, on the east side of the Cascade range, to which field we shall now turn our attention.

On the 26th of March last Colonel Wright, in command, left Fort Dalles for the Walla-Walla country, having withdrawn from the Cascades all the defence except the sergeant and nine men, in charge of the block-house, and encamped five miles beyond Fort Dalles. He was now fifty miles to the east of the Cascades, (map 19.)

On the same day (March 26, 1856,) the Indians attacked the Cascades and took the place, all but the block-house, which was gallantly defended by Sergeant Kelly with eight men, who had one killed and two wounded.

On the same night an express reached Colonel Wright, who immediately countermarched; also one reached Fort Vancouver, from which Lieutenant Sheridan, 4th infantry, with a detachment, was sent up, which reached the foot of the Cascades 9 o'clock the morning of the 27th and engaged the Indians; but, finding them too strong, drew off and sent to Fort Vancouver for a reinforcement.

On the morning of the 8th Colonel Wright, with a force of 250 rank and file, landed under the fire from the Indians at the head of the Cascades and drove them. Then a detachment advanced under Brevet Lieutenant Colonel Steptoe, major 9th infantry, and drove the Indians, relieved the block-house, and was joined by Lieutenant Sheridan's detachment, and soon retook the whole line (about $4\frac{1}{2}$ miles) of the Cascades. They lost three killed and had three wounded, in course of the 26th, 27th, and 28th, in this affair. Besides these, the Indians killed thirteen white men, women, and children, in their attack on the Cascades the first day. Several Indians were killed by the troops on this occasion.

It appeared in evidence that the chief, Chimoneth, and eight of his men, supposed to be friendly, of the band who lived there, were guilty of co-operating in this attack on the Cascades; these were executed. It subsequently appeared that the Klikatats were the principal actors in this attack, which was instigated by Kamiakin, chief of the Yakamas, whose plan was to take the Cascades, destroy the steamers above and below, and sweep the Columbia of every white inhabitant.

Colonel Wright built two block-houses—one at the foot and one at the head of the Cascades—which, with the small garrison left in them, afforded ample protection afterwards.

About the 6th of April General Wool, accompanied by his aid, Lieutenant Arnold, Lieutenants Colonel Nauman and Ripley, left Benicia for the Columbia River district, and the general ascended to Fort Dalles, arriving there in time to give Colonel Wright further instructions in reference to operations in the Yakama country, which consisted in moving promptly an expedition of five companies into that field from Fort Dalles, (map 17.)

On the 28th of April this command had crossed the Columbia from Fort Dalles. Previous to starting, Colonel Wright addressed the governor of Oregon as follows:

"I am much embarrassed by these wanton attacks of the Oregon volunteers on the friendly Indians. Under these circumstances, and presuming that you still retain authority over the Oregon volunteers, although at present beyond your territorial jurisdiction, I have to request that they may be withdrawn from the country on the north side of the Columbia river."

Frequent official letters had been received from the Indian agents in charge of these friendly Indians, as also of those towards the Walla-Walla, complaining of the outrages committed by the volunteers, (Nesmith's command,) and asking for regular troops to be stationed in certain places to protect them against the volunteers.

Colonel Wright had advanced into the Yakama country, and was encamped on the Natchess river 18th May, (map 17.) At that time the river was so high that it was impassable. On the opposite (north) side the main body of the Yakama Indians were collected in very considerable numbers, expressing a desire for peace. To this end the talks were held.

The chiefs, Ow-hi and Te-i-as, had promised on the 11th June to come in with their people in five days. Since that time, up to the 18th June, no Indians, however, had come in, and Colonel Wright had no information of their whereabouts, all having left the north side of the river.

A bridge having been completed on the morning of the 18th June, Colonel Wright crossed the Natchess with eight companies—450 rank and file—and marched north over a broken country and encamped on the Wenass river. Lieutenant Colonel Steptoe was left, with three companies, to occupy Fort Natchess. On 20th June Colonel Wright was encamped in the Kittetas valley without having found the Indians. He says: "I do not despair of ultimately reducing these Indians to sue for peace. I believe they really desire it, and I must find out what outside influence is operating to keep them from coming in."

The governor of Washington had organized a battalion of volunteers, under Lieutenant Colonel B. F. Shaw, which left Camp Montgomery (map 16) 12th June, passed through Natchess Pass, and encamped 20th June on the Wenass, (map 17.) It will be perceived that this battalion of volunteers entered the Yakama country in the rear of Colonel Wright's command, just after they had left the Wenass for the north.

Colonel Wright had, before Shaw started, declined all co-operation with these volunteers, and informed him (Shaw) that he had an ample force of regulars for operations in the Yakama country.

The probability is, that the knowledge of the approach of Shaw's battalion had caused the Indians to disperse and deterred them from coming in as they had agreed. Colonel Wright says: "I have not overlooked, from the first, the evident determination of the volunteers to co-operate with the regular forces to bring this war to a close, and I have steadily resisted all advances. My efforts have been retarded but not defeated by what was done."

On the 18th July, 1856, Colonel Wright reports, "that, notwithstanding the numerous difficulties and embarrassments I have encountered, the war in this country is closed. We have penetrated the most remote hiding-places of the enemy and forced him to ask for mercy. Deserted by their chiefs, Kameakin and Ow-hi, and perseveringly pursued by our troops, the Indians have no other course left them but to surrender. So long as troops simply moved through their country and retired it had little effect; the Indians were generally the gainers by it. But a steady advance over their whole country, rendering it necessary to move their stock and families, had a different effect, understanding, as they do, that the country is to be permanently occupied.''

From the 16th to the 30th June the governor of Washington was at Fort Dalles, giving his orders for the operation of the volunteers. He ordered Shaw, 20th June, to move his battalion from the Winass and ''push on to Walla-Walla, unite his force with that moving from the Dalles, and take the command of the whole.'' The force at the Dalles moved June 25. Both columns contained 360 enlisted men and about 100 employés. These volunteers arrived at Mill Creek, Walla-Walla valley, on 8th July.

On the 2d August the general commanding the department of the Pacific issued the following order to Colonel Wright: ''The general congratulates you on your successful termination of the war with the Yakamas and Klikitats. * * * The general desires you, with the least possible delay, to conduct an expedition into the Walla-Walla country. Having arranged all difficulties with those tribes, then establish the post, as before directed, in the Walla-Walla country. No emigrants or other whites, except the Hudson Bay Company, or persons having ceded rights from the Indians, will be permitted to settle or remain in the Indian country or on land not ceded by treaty, confirmed by the Senate, and approved by the President of the United States, excepting the miners at the Colville mines. These will be notified, however, that if they interfere with the Indians or their squaws they will be punished and sent out of the country. It appears that Colonel Shaw, from Puget's Sound, with his volunteers, has gone to the Walla-Walla country. Colonel Wright will order them out of the country by way of Fort Dalles. If they do not go immediately they will be arrested, disarmed, and sent out.''

Lieutenant Colonel Steptoe, with four companies, started from Fort Dalles 20th August for the Walla-Walla valley, and reached there about the last of the month. Governor Stevens had preceded him.

On the 14th August the governor reports to the Secretary of War: ''I expressed the opinion that the indecisive and procrastinating course pursuing and pursued in the Yakama country had brought or nearly brought about a general combination of tribes eastward. That combination I hoped to break up. The Walla-Walla expedition has been completely successful. Colonel Shaw learning there was a large force of hostiles in the Grand Rond, determined to attack them. Moving in the night of 14th July he struck them on the 17th, and after a running fight of 15 miles he entirely defeated them, captured a large number of animals, destroyed nearly all of their provisions, and also got possession of about 100 pounds of their ammunition. The loss of the enemy was at least 40 killed on the field of battle.

"I push forward in person to Walla-Walla to-morrow to meet the Indians and establish relations of friendship with the tribes generally, and especially those struck by Lieut. Col. Shaw."

Now, by comparing the dates of the operations of Col. Wright in the Yakama country, it will be perceived how unjust is the reflection made upon him by the executive of Washington Territory, for Col. Wright's forces had advanced into and had the occupancy of that country six weeks at least before the governor's volunteers started for the same. With regard to the boasted strike of Col. Shaw upon the Indians at Grand Rond, which his excellency seems to take pleasure in reporting to the Secretary of War, let us here record what "Howlish Wampum," the Cayuse chief, says about it. He says: "When Col. Shaw arrived in this valley I went to see him. Col. Shaw said to me that he had come to make peace; that he had thrown his arms behind him. I told him my heart was made happy. Soon after Col. Shaw marched for the Grand Rond. The Cayuses were encamped there—that is, the women, old men, and children, with a few of the young men. The chiefs were absent when Col. Shaw approached. We sent Captain 'John,' a friendly Nez Percé, to talk with the Cayuses. No persons authorized to talk were in the Cayuse camp. The women and children became alarmed at the advance of the volunteers, and commenced packing up. The volunteers then charged the camp and killed several old men, women and children."

With regard to the credibility of this chief I have only to say, he is the man the Oregon volunteers produced as their witness in justification of their acts in the Walla-Walla valley.

In reference to the part of his report where the governor says, "he goes forward to the Walla-Walla to meet the Indians and establish relations of friendship with the tribes generally," we shall see that his mission was anything but successful, and it was not his plan of military operations after all that closed the war in that valley.

This plan was promulgated to the Secretary of War, dated May 23, 1856, in which it is said: "I cannot too strongly urge the policy of accumulating supplies in the Yakama country and in the Walla-Walla, in readiness to wage a winter campaign. With proper preparation a winter campaign can be waged and the war ended."

A small pack train despatched by George Stevens for Walla-Walla, in advance of Steptoe's command, was captured by Indians, said to have been of the tribes attacked by Shaw at the Grand Rond, in July. The governor, as superintendent of Indian affairs, was taking up a supply of provisions and presents for the Indians, with whom he expected to hold a council about the time of the arrival of Steptoe's command.

On the 15th September this superintendent of Indian affairs was holding a council in the immediate neighborhood of Col. Steptoe's camp, on mill creek. There were some four thousand present, embracing the Nez Percés, Cayuses, Walla-Wallas, and the bands of

Kamiakin, Schloom, and Ow-hi Yakamas. The Indians visited Col. Steptoe in person, and he was quite successful in restoring their confidence in the white people, which was much shaken by the recent conduct of the volunteers, who now had been disbanded and were en route for Fort Dalles.

On the 18th September, Steptoe reports: "I attended the council yesterday, and was satisfied Governor Stevens had effected no good by assembling the tribes. The governor admitted to me to-day he had failed to accomplish what he had hoped, but he charged his failure to want of support from the regular army."

"I cannot help feeling gratified that the treaty of Walla-Walla has not yet been ratified, because it is plain to me that an attempt to execute it now would be attended by resistance at once on the part of most of the Nez Percés, and ultimately by combined resistance among the surrounding tribes. I must confess that, in my judgment, it is unfortunate that Governor Stevens should have appointed this as the time for holding his council," &c.

After the council had broken up, 19th September, the Nez Perces had most of them started for their homes, and the governor's party for Fort Dalles. By the time the latter had gone three miles from Steptoe's camp, his party was attacked, and he sent back a note to Steptoe for aid, saying "he had 250 Indians in front." This note was received by Steptoe at sunset, 19th. The colonel suggested to the governor to fall back with his party to his camp, and they would then go to the Umatilla, to which he would move his camp, and where he could give protection. To this the governor replied in another note: "It is impossible for me to move back without assistance. We have around us 300 Indians. Send your dragoons and a portion of Fletcher's company as soon as possible, and I will go back to your camp." This was received by Steptoe at 11 o'clock that night, and he immediately sent a force with orders "to attack the Indians surrounding the governor's party, and bring it to camp." This duty was handsomely performed by the regulars. The party was rescued and safely brought to camp by 4 o'clock the next morning. On the return they were assailed, but the Indians were promptly driven by the regulars without sustaining any loss. The rescuing party was officered by Lieuts. Davidson and Wickliffe.

A block house was erected at Mill creek, and the remainder of the command moved to the Umatilla, where grass could be obtained for the animals, that about the creek having been burnt by the Indians.

On the 19th October the general directed Col. Wright to proceed in person to the Walla-Walla as soon as possible, to attend to the establishment of the post, as before directed, in that vicinity, and sent Captain (Brevet Major) Wyse's company, 3d artillery, to reinforce his command, which took post at the Cascades.

"It is also of the highest importance that you, the senior officer, (the chief man,) should see and talk with all the tribes in that region, in order to ascertain their wants, feelings and disposition towards the whites. Warned by what has occurred, the general trusts you will be on your guard against the whites, and adopt the most prompt and vigorous measures to crush the enemy before they have time to combine for resistance, check the war, and prevent further trouble by keeping the whites out of the Indian country."

On the 30th and 31st October Colonel Wright reports from the Walla-Walla valley as follows: "I have selected this position on Mill creek, 6 miles above its junction with the Walla-Walla river, for the post."

After the council of Governor Stevens (in September) the Indians dispersed, and it has been a work of great difficulty to communicate with them. Many are so remote that it is impossible to communicate with them. I have, however, in my camp, about 40. I have had several talks with them; all very satisfactory. From appearances I apprehend no serious difficulties with any of these Indians. The council of Governor Stevens was unfortunate; the Indians, many of them, are hostile to him. They are opposed to the Walla-Walla treaty of 1855, which he made with them, and will never be contented until it is restored to them. I am fully satisfied it should not be confirmed.

"On assembling in council yesterday, I stated to them, that I wished to have a full and frank expression of their feelings and dispositions towards the whites; the causes which brought on the war, &c. There were present the chiefs Red Wolf, Eagle from the Light, Howlish Wampum, Tinton Metey, Stickees, two sons of Looking-Glass, besides several sub-chiefs and headmen of Nez Percés and Cayuse nations."

The chiefs said, "it was Laywer and his people who sold the country at the Walla-Walla treaty of 1855, our hearts have been crying ever since, we did not wish to sell our lands. The hearts of the Indians were bad from that time. The first drop of blood that was shed was caused by that treaty."

"The speeches of all the chiefs amounted to the same as this. They all denounced the treaty; both the Cayuses and Nez Percés were very severe on Lawyer and his party, whom they accuse of having been brought over."

Eagle of the Light was sent by Looking Glass, the war chief of the Nez Percés, as his representative, whose views in relation to the treaty were the same as the other chiefs, and he attributed to it the first shedding of blood. He said, "he understood that Colonel Wright came here to straighten out things, and wished to know whether the bloody cloth was to be washed and made white, and all that is past forgotten, or whether the war was to be continued between the whites and red men. For his part he was for peace. He desired to see the good talk of the white chiefs and the Indian planted in good soil and grow up together. He desired to live in peace and harmony with the white people."

Colonel Wright replied: "That the bloody cloth should be washed, not a spot should be left upon it. That the Great Spirit had created both the white and red men, and commanded us to 'love one another,' that all past differences must be thrown behind us, that the hatchet must be buried, and that for the future perpetual friendship must exist between us; that the good talk we had this day listened to should be planted and grow up in our hearts and drive away all bad feelings, and preserve peace and friendship between us forever. I told them to put what I said in their hearts, and when they returned to their homes to repeat it to all their friends."

Colonel Wright reported the foregoing to the general, and adds: "I am fully satisfied with all that has been said, peace and quiet can easy be maintained. The Indians are perfectly satisfied with the establishment of a military post here. All they want is quiet and protection. I must express my decided opposition to the treaty of Walla-Walla, and pray it may never be confirmed. All the chiefs in this and the Yakama country whom I have seen are violently opposed to it. Give them back those treaties and no cause of war exists. They proclaim that unfair means were used, whether so or not they will not be contented until these treaties are restored."

On hearing of what had been done by Colonel Wright, the superintendent of Indian affairs for Washington says to the Secretary of War. "I now make the direct issue with Colonel Wright that he has made a concession to the Indians which he had no right to make, that by so doing he has done nothing but to get the semblance of a peace, and that by his acts he has in a measure weakened the influence of the department having the authority to make treaties and having the charge of the friendly Indians. He has, in my judgment, abandoned his own duty, which was to reduce the Indians to submission, and has trenched upon and usurped a portion of mine."

The United States Steamer Massasuchetts, Captain Swartwout, at the request of Lieutenant Colonel Casey, pursued a band of northern Indians of about 117 in number, who had come down in their war canoes, and depredated at various points. They were found November 20, encamped at Fort Gamble, and after giving them battle they were received on board and transported to Victoria, under a promise that they would never return again. About 27 of the Indians were killed and all their canoes and property destroyed before they would surrender.

This descent of the northern Indians was more for the purpose of plundering the Puget's Sound Indians than the whites. There was no intention on their part to war upon the whites. They had before been driven away from Steilacoom by the troops there, and had been worsted in a fight with some Indians on one of the reservations in the sound.

On the 18th of December, 1856, the commanding general of the department of the Pacific reported: "The mail has arrived from Oregon, bringing the gratifying intelligence from Colonel Wright and Lieut. Colonel Casey that all is peace and quiet in the two Territories, Oregon and Washington.

"Under present arrangements, I don't believe that the war can be renewed by the whites. The posts are well arranged to preserve peace and to protect the inhabitants from any hostility on the part of the Indians residing in the Territories."

X.—*Military considerations in reference to the California portion of the Department of the Pacific.*

In the preceding chapter, IX, it has been said that while the troops were actively engaged in suppressing hostilities in the northern portions of the department an Indian war was threatened in certain portions of California.

The causes which led to this state of things, and the measures taken to meet the exigency, will be briefly narrated in the present chapter.

On the Colorado river, a bitter feud existed between the people of two tribes which was constantly likely to break out into overt acts. Brevet Lieut. Colonel Nauman, 3d artillery, was dispatched to Fort Yuma in January, 1856, for the purpose of inquiring into the troubles there apprehended. His mission was productive of good results; he satisfied himself that there was no combination between these tribes and those further north. The report of Lieutenant Colonel Nauman gives some practical suggestions of importance in reference to the appointment of an Indian agent to reside permanently at Fort Yuma, for the purpose of controlling these Indians.

In the month of January, 1856, Captain Burton, 3d artillery, commanding at San Diego, was instructed to visit the tribes in the neighborhood with a command from his post, with a view of restoring quiet among them, and ascertaining the causes of the difficulties, (map 7.)

This expedition resulted favorably, and it appeared that the encroachment of the whites upon the lands set apart by treaty for the Indians, the neglect of the Indian agents to supply them with the articles stipulated in the treaty, and the stealing of the cattle of the whites, by some of the Indians, were the principal sources of the apprehended outbreaks. Captain Burton became satisfied that the principal chief of the Carvilla Indians had endeavored to form a combination with the Mohaves and Yumas, for the purpose of attacking the white settlements in this neighborhood, during the preceding autumn, but failed; and the captain attributed the failure to the prompt movement of the troops in the preceding November.

The Carvilla Indians occupy the country from San Gorgonia Pass to the Arroyo Blanco, (map 6.) Captain Burton proceeded to that district in April, 1856, and ascertained that the whites were in the habit of encroaching on the grounds set apart for these people, and that this, and the thefts of those Indians who were without food, were the causes of the apprehended outbreaks; and he obtained evidence of two leading Mormons of San Bernardino having, in the autumn of 1855, sent the following message to these Indians: "The Mormons and Indians are friends; the Americans are the enemies of the Mormons and Indians, and had hitherto driven both from the great waters of the east."

It is also in evidence that Nathan C. Kinney, bishop of the Mormon church in San Bernardino, in the month of May, 1856, visited these Indians and called them together and admonished them as follows:

"The Americans are a bad people, were not Christians, and were the enemies of the Mormons, and not to be relied on or believed in nowise, for the Americans are fools and devils; and that the Mormons were the rulers of the country and not the Americans, and that he (Bishop Kinney) proposed to gather the Indians into the Mormon settlement of San Bernardino, and there to maintain them; and that the Mormons were not Americans, but a different people; and that he came to baptize the Indians into the Mormon church."

There is other evidence to show that this same bishop instructed the Indians to kill the whites who were not Mormons, and that he would reward them with the cattle and horses of the whites.

To the judicious action of Captain Burton, under the orders he received from the general commanding the department, we are in a great measure indebted for the peace we were afterwards permitted to enjoy in that quarter.

Reports had been brought to the commanding general of the department that the United States land surveying parties in the Mohave river district (map 6) had been attacked and several killed by the Indians, and he was called upon to send a military force there to protect the surveying parties.

On the 8th April, 1856, instructions were issued to the commanding officer at Fort Tejon to send a company of dragoons from that post into the Mohave river country; but when it was on the point of starting a threatened outbreak, reported by the Indian agent of the Tejon (St. Sebastian) reservation, (map 5,) made it expedient to postpone the expedition and send the troops to the reservation. In the mean time it was ascertained that the United States land surveyors who had been at work in the Mohave country were safe and the Indians there were quiet.

On the 1st May, 1856, the commanding officer at Fort Miller reported that in the Tulare valley, in the latter part of April, "some Indians had killed a cow belonging to a white man; some of the citizens (about two-thirds) wished to demand the aggressors of the chiefs, but the minority portion insisted upon punishing all the Indians collectively, and for this purpose had organized themselves and gone in pursuit, but returned soon after with the report that 500 warriors had made a stand. The next day these whites attacked a friendly party of Indians, who had remained neutral, and killed six, wounded several, and the others dispersed. Another party of friendly Indians shared a similar fate. From these facts, that officer says: "The number of hostile Indians, therefore, encamped at the head of the Tulare valley (map 5) may not be overrated."

It is due to the citizens to say that the "war party of whites" was only about one-third of the whole population; but the "war party" called upon the governor for aid, and he called on the commanding officer of the department. In the mean time a detachment of regulars from Fort Miller, under Lieutenant Livingston, 3d artillery, and one from Fort Tejon, under Lieutenant Alston, 1st dragoons, had been sent into the field of those disturbances.

The general caused the following reply to be sent to the governor:

"Detachments from both Fort Miller and Fort Tejon are now in the field, and no doubt would be able to preserve peace, were it not from the determination of a few designing white men, as it would appear, to wage a war of extermination against the Indians. "No additional force of regulars can be sent to the Tulare at this time, nearly all being now in the field against hostile Indians in Oregon and Washington, and in the northern part of California. * * * We have yet to learn that the Indians have struck a blow against the whites in the Tulare except in self defence; and the general is of the opinion that the regular force in the southeastern part of the State is sufficient to protect the settlers from Indian aggressions, provided the frequent murders and aggressions on the part of the whites against the Indians are checked before the latter are driven to combine in a general war against the former."

The war party, however, obtained arms, and organized themselves into companies of volunteers, and in two engagements were repulsed by the Indians, who had fortified themselves in a strong position.

On the 13th May, 1856, Lieutenant Livingston, having been furnished with a howitzer, went with 20 regulars and about 30 volunteers to reconnoitre the position, and while so doing the lieutenant became satisfied that an immediate attack would prove successful. He accordingly turned their position, attacked them in flank, and drove them before him, killing many and destroying their camp and provisions. This was near the "Four Creeks." After this the Indians fled and dispersed in the recesses of the Sierra Nevada mountains. The volunteers, the "war party" of the whites, soon became tired and returned to their homes.

The activity of the regulars under Lieutenants Livingston and Alston, put the inhabitants of the Tulare valley out of any further danger.

The governor of California, much to his credit, in furnishing these volunteers with the arms sent him by General Wool for their own defence, directed them to incur no expense except for the transportation of the arms, and explicitly prohibited them from proceeding against the Indians, but to come to terms as soon as possible.

XI.—*Superintendents of Indian affairs; Indian sub-agents; military commanders of posts in Indian countries; Indian reservations.*

The commanders of military posts in the Indian countries have been stripped of all functions pertaining to Indian agencies, to the end of assigning these to civilians, whose chief aim in accepting them can only be to make profit of the appointments; in many cases, it is feared, regardless of justice to the Indian or to the government.

To such Indian sub-agencies the troops have been humbled to the condition, too often, of "hewers of wood and drawers of water," or of acting only as a police "posse."

It is a glaring fact that army detachments on the frontiers are frequently called upon to quell Indian hostilities either originated by designing agents themselves, or caused through ignorance, indifference, or complicity, to be fomented by bad citizens into actual war.

So long as the present policy obtains of dividing the administration of the practical operations, in reference to the tribes, between a Commissioner of Indian Affairs and a Secretary of War, without subjecting the former to the authority of the latter, just so long will inefficiency pervade the system.

The present practice of separating all control over the sub-agents from the commanding officers of posts, and lodging it in the hands of superintendents of Indian affairs, who are under the direction of a civil bureau, inefficient in the matter, because of its want of military organization and military authority, can never be otherwise than injurious, on the whole, to the Indian service.

As good may come of evil, so, undoubtedly, there are a few cases under the present rule that may work well. But these cases are the exceptions to the rule.

Under the existing policy there is seldom any cordial co-operation between the agents of the War Department and those of the Department of the Interior upon Indian matters when in the act of executing orders in the field. The Indian bureau should never have been severed from the War Department, and the sooner it is restored by act of Congress to its former and most natural parent the better will it be for those truly interested in the rightful ends of government.

Colonel Wright, 9th infantry, while in the Walla-Walla country reported his views upon this subject, which accord so entirely with my own observations that I here quote them :

"During a long service I have had much to do with Indians, and the opinion which I have ever entertained has been that their entire management should be in the hands of the War Department. The interest of the Indians, alike with that of the government, demands it. The Indian department cannot control the Indians without the aid of the military. The Indians will be much better satisfied. They will not be embarrassed by conflicting counsels. They will know what to rely upon. If we expect the Indians to put faith in us we must have a unity and singleness of purpose. This can only be accomplished under the jurisdiction of one white chief."

Indian wars on our frontiers will never cease to be brought on by bad white people until commanding officers of posts are clothed with authority to arrest and bring to trial white depredators in the Indian countries, and on the Indian reserves, before proper tribunals.

Practically, under the existing system, if a white man murder an Indian the murderer is entitled to trial by jury before being hung, and all his family are not necessarily included in his doom. But if an Indian commit the venial offence of stealing a white man's pig, to keep himself from starving, the case is quite different; "it is your bull that has gored my ox;" and forthwith a war of extermination is declared and vigorously prosecuted against the whole band to which the Indian belongs, and wo be unto the popularity of a commanding officer who should presume to raise his voice against the indiscriminate slaughter.

The provisions of the existing laws of Congress ("Act to regulate trade and intercourse with Indian tribes, &c., passed 23d Congress, 1st session, approved June 30, 1834, and its amendatory act, 29th Congress, 2d session, approved March 3, 1847,") are severe enough. But are they executed? No. This is a dead letter in practice, inoperative in the hands of civil agents, and it is over-ridden by an act of the Oregon legislature! The statute of this Territory sets at nought and declares the statute of Congress a nullity in reference to this intercourse. And while an officer is compelled to execute a law of Congress he makes himself amenable to the law of Oregon. And here we have the reason why the hostile Indians are found so well armed and appointed for war. The in moving whites sell their rifles, revolvers, and ammunition to the Indians, because they get large prices; and the traffic is unrestrained, because said law of Congress is null, in virtue of the Oregon law, which is such as to remove all chance of proof against the culprit. At the battle of Big Meadows, on Rogue river, the Indians were armed with the best of Sharp's rifles and Colt's revolvers, sold to them by the whites; and it was on account of the inferiority of the arms, which his men had to use by an absurd regulation, that Captain Smith came so near losing that battle.

The system of colonizing the Indians within the limits of a State or Territory upon reservations is, perhaps, under all circumstances, the most humane, economical, and practicable that can be adopted. But to render this effective two things are essentially necessary, but which are too often neglected by the Indian department :

1. It is essential to survey the reservation and mark it out on the ground by metes and bounds so that the Indian and the white may know its exact limits. It is too commonly the case that the reservation is but a mere paper reservation; no survey having been made, no bounds or monuments set to mark its existence, or to show where jurisdiction begins or ends.

2. There should be a competent military force stationed on the reservation. It has become quite too much the practice to leave these reservations unguarded by any military force, and to wait until difficulties occur between the Indians on them and the encroaching whites, and then, after the troubles begin, to send for the military to suppress the outbreak, whereas the practice should be to have a sufficient force at all times immediately on the spot to prevent encroachments and to enforce obedience.

All of which, general, is most respectfully submitted by your very obedient servant,

THO. JEFFERSON CRAM,
Captain U. S. T. E.

Major General JOHN E. WOOL,
United States Army.

HEADQUARTERS DEPARTMENT OF THE EAST,
Troy, N. Y., January 2, 1858.

SIR: Herewith I have the honor to transmit, through the headquarters of the army, a very able, interesting, and truthful memoir and report, with maps, by Captain T. J. Cram, of the Topographical Engineers, of the topography and military operations of the department of the Pacific whilst under my command in 1854, 1855, 1856, and 1857.

In presenting the memoir and report I would respectfully call attention to the following subjects, viz:

First. Chapters one and two, which contain a general description of the department of the Pacific, including the ocean front.

Second. Chapter three, pages 36 to 43, refers to an arsenal of construction and depot for quartermaster and commissary supplies at Benicia, California. The suggestions of Captain Cram I think ought to be adopted.

Third. Chapters four and five refer to roads, routes, and distances. The route from New York and New Orleans, *via* Panama, San Francisco, and Sacramento, to Utah, or Salt Lake City, may be considered of sufficient importance to claim special notice. I would simply add that a military expedition from Sacramento, on account of snow in the mountain passes, would be impracticable in the winter season.—(See pages 97 to 113.)

Fourth. Chapter six is interesting, having reference to the wars between the whites and Indians in Oregon, by a perusal of which it will be seen that the whites have generally been the aggressors. In the same chapter will be discovered the diabolical character of Ben Wright, Indian sub-agent, who has been represented in Congress as the friend of the Indians.—(See pages 141 to 155.)

Fifth. The Indian war in Rogue River valley in 1855 and 1856.—(See pages 156 to 190, in which will be discovered the immediate causes of the war, its results, and the gallant and efficient manner by which the war was brought to a close by the regular troops, under the command of Lieutenant Colonel Buchanan.)

Sixth. Pages 197 to 228 give an accurate description of the country, its roads, rivers, and distances, embraced in western, northern, and eastern Oregon.

Seventh. In chapter seven, pages 229 to 281, will be found an interesting description of Washington Territory, and particularly of Puget's Sound. The military posts, roads, and improvements recommended for this Territory I deem no less necessary to secure the peace of the country than for the defence and protection of the inhabitants. A steamer of the speed of at least ten to twelve miles the hour is required in Puget's Sound for the protection of the whites and Indians against the marauding Indians of the English and Russian possessions.

Eighth. Chapter eight relates to Indian treaties. In pages 252 to

315 will be discovered the causes of the war and its continuance in Washington Territory. The truthful history of Governor Stevens' efforts to form treaties with the Indian tribes in his Territory, which were not at the time called for, I would recommend as worthy of the perusal of the Secretary of War.

Ninth. Chapter nine, pages 316 to 433, furnishes an interesting history of the several expeditions against the Yakamas, of the war in Puget's Sound, and of Governor Curry's most wanton, illegal, and uncalled for expedition against the Walla-Wallas, and the similar expedition of Colonel Shaw against the Cayuses. The expedition against the Walla-Walla Indians was an effort on the part of Governor Curry to bring on a war that would be of long continuance, in the expectation of a large drain from the treasury of the United States. Although the war did not continue as long as the governor anticipated, he, no doubt, will present an account that will, if approved by Congress, take from the treasury of the United States several millions of dollars. Congress, however, may hesitate to appropriate to the full amount claimed, from the fact that the expenses incurred were paid in territorial scrip, much of which has been sold for less than twenty-five cents on the dollar.

On a careful examination of the conduct of Governor Curry and others in carrying on the war it will be, I think, discovered that it was not so much to protect and defend the inhabitants from Indian barbarities as it was to promote ambitious and speculating schemes. One thing is certain, that powers greater than belong to the President were exerted to carry on the war, by fitting out expeditions against the Walla-Wallas and the Cayuses, which were wholly unnecessary and under no circumstances called for, the expenses of which, no doubt, will swell the claim against the United States one or two millions, perhaps more. If Congress should foot the bill, which, it is said, will amount to more than six millions, I would not be surprised if the next territorial Indian war should cost ten or twelve millions. I do not know how this question of governors of Territories making war on their own account, and beyond their own jurisdiction, will be considered. If countenanced by the government, I would not be surprised if the example should, when least expected, and that time may have already arrived, lead to embarrassing results, at least in regard to the finances of the government. It appears to me that governors of Territories should not be permitted to make war on their own account and beyond their own jurisdiction.

Tenth. Chapter eleven, page 445, relates to superintendents of Indian affairs, which is especially recommended to the attention of the Secretary of War. The affairs of the Indian department as hitherto conducted in the department of the Pacific have been of very slight, if any, advantage to the Indians; whilst for their benefit large amounts have been drawn from the treasury of the United States. The superintendency of the Indians should, beyond all question, be under the control of the War Department.

Having thus called attention to some of the most important subjects contained in Captain Cram's memoir and report, I would add that it is due to him to say that he has on all occasions whilst under my command exhibited talents, zeal, ability, and efficiency worthy of the highest commendation.

I have the honor to be, very respectfully, your obedient servant,

JOHN E. WOOL,
Major General.

Hon. JOHN B. FLOYD,
Secretary of War.

HARD
CIDER